J. Stewart Stein
CONSTRUCTION GLOSSARY: AN ENCYCLOPEDIC REFERENCE
AND MANUAL

James E. Clyde
CONSTRUCTION INSPECTION: A FIELD GUIDE TO PRACTICE

Harold J. Rosen and Philip M. Bennett
CONSTRUCTION MATERIALS EVALUATION AND SELE~~~~~ A
SYSTEMATIC APPROACH

CONSTRUCTION MATERIALS EVALUATION AND SELECTION

During 1974 Phil Bennett of the University of Wisconsin-Extension conceived the idea of a short course that would explore the critical choices to be made in selecting building products and materials. After exploring the possibilities with Harold Rosen, an investigation was made of various studies in the field of performance requirements and checklists of material characteristics.

A format was developed for a course entitled "A Systematic Approach to Building Material Evaluation and Selection." The course is based on a recommended checklist of attributes or characteristics to be investigated using performance analysis and/or judgmental values. To flesh out the course, it was proposed that the concept could best be presented by reviewing those materials that are generally involved in trade sections that are included under Divisions 2 through 9 of the CSI Format.

A six-day short course was originated in 1975 with the assistance of 21 instructors who are expert in the various materials and systems that are normally associated with Divisions 2 through 9. Sessions cover site work, concrete, masonry, metals, wood, thermal and moisture protection, doors and windows, and building finishes.

This book, however, deals only with the basic concept of materials evaluation and selection and sets forth a recommended procedure that can be utilized by the design professional, the contractor, and the construction manager. In addition, the concept can be utilized by the building materials manufacturer to test and report on those characteristics that are pertinent to the product.

The authors wish to acknowledge the beneficial critiques of the manuscript by Justin Heinlein of Turner Construction Co., Joseph P. Welsh of Haywood Baker Co., and Charles Parise of Smith, Hinchman & Grylis, Assoc. Inc.

CONSTRUCTION MATERIALS EVALUATION AND SELECTION
A SYSTEMATIC APPROACH

HAROLD J. ROSEN, P. E.
Merrick, New York

PHILIP M. BENNETT, R. A.

Associate Professor
Department of Engineering
University of Wisconsin—Extension
Madison, Wisconsin

A Wiley-Interscience Publication

JOHN WILEY & SONS
New York   Chichester   Brisbane   Toronto

Library of Congress Cataloging in Publication Data

Rosen, Harold J.
    Construction materials evaluation and selection.

    (Wiley series of practical construction guides)
    "A Wiley-Interscience publication."
    Bibliography: p.
    Includes index.
    1. Building materials.   I.   Bennett, Philip M.,
1936–   II.   Title.

TA403.R569   691   79-15885
ISBN 0-471-73565-5

Printed in the United States of America

10 9 8 7 6 5 4 3 2 1

Series Preface

The Wiley Series of Practical Construction Guides provides the working constructor with up-to-date information that can help to increase the job profit margin. These guidebooks, which are mainly for practice, but include the necessary theory and design, should aid a construction contractor in approaching work problems with more knowledgeable confidence. The guides should be useful also to engineers, architects, planners, specification writers, project managers, superintendents, materials and equipment manufacturers, and, the source of all these callings, instructors and their students.

Construction in the United States alone will reach $250 billion a year in the early 1980s. In all nations, the business of building will continue to grow at a phenomenal rate, because the population proliferation demands new living, working, and recreational facilities. This construction will have to be more substantial, thus demanding a more professional performance from the contractor. Before science and technology had seriously affected the ideas, job plans, financing, and erection of structures, most contractors developed their know-how by field trial-and-error. Wheels, small and large, were constantly being reinvented in all sectors, because there was no interchange of knowledge. The current complexity of construction, even in more rural areas, has revealed a clear need for more proficient, professional methods and tools in both practice and learning.

Because construction is highly competitive, some practical technology is necessarily proprietary. But most practical day-to-day problems are common to the whole construction industry. These are the subjects for the Wiley Practical Construction Guide.

M. D. MORRIS, P. E.

New York, New York

Preface

Need for a Rational Analytical Approach

There are several categories of individuals associated with the construction process who require a more rational approach to the evaluation and selection of building products. They can be identified and their area of responsibility pinpointed as follows:

1. *Architect and Engineer.* The design professional must evaluate and select building products for use in a project.
2. *Construction Manager.* The construction phase expert must make recommendations on building products to bring a project in at the construction cost estimate.
3. *Subcontractor.* The specialist in a building trade becomes a licensed applicator or exponent of specific products.
4. *Building Materials Manufacturer.* The developer of a product who must provide adequate information in the form of product literature.

What is the process employed today by the user in evaluating a new product, material, or system introduced by a building materials manufacturer? There are any number of answers; none, however, is predicated on some rational methodology or scientific investigation that provides for a comprehensive analysis.

When one looks back at the number of materials that were available to the design professional at the beginning of this century one can readily discern the enormous disparity that presently exists over what was available then. In 1906 when Sweets published their first Architectural file of manufacturers catalogs, it consisted of a single volume. That single volume contained approximately 150 to 200 manufacturers at most, and this comprised all or most of the building product materials known at that time.

Today the quantity of manufacturers literature concerning building products available to the design professional is enormous in terms of the number of manufacturers and the number of pages of manufacturers literature. As a matter of fact, there are now 13 Sweets Catalogs in the Architectural File with approximately 18,000 to 20,000 pages in these bound volumes. When the film libraries are examined, such as IDAC, VSMF, and Showcase, we find that they have compiled libraries of architectural, mechanical, and electrical products that comprise approximately some 5000 manufacturers.

When design professionals or specifiers finally review product literature, on what basis do they determine how to evaluate the product? Just what do they do today?

For example if the product literature emanates from a company of major standing in the country or a national company, is the product therefore assumed to be good? Is the determination made because the design professional knows the particular manufacturer's representative? Both those factors can result in a wrong decision.

When a design professional is introduced to a new product by a sales representative who delivers a sales pitch and product literature, what kind of questions does the design professional formulate to assess the quality of the product? In the short time available for a sales call the design professional who has no prior knowledge of the product and the benefit of some organized assessment procedure, flounders about asking questions that come to mind at the moment, overlooking some salient questions that might be quite pertinent.

Testing Samples in the Office

Another completely unorthodox procedure indulged in by many prospective users, either because (1) they don't have any money to invest in a laboratory investigation or (2) they simply are not equipped by virtue of their education and experience to comprehend scientific investigation, is to subject the product or a sample to the following office test procedures:

1. Flex a corner until it breaks or tears.
2. Put a match to it.
3. Drop it from waist height to the floor.
4. Soak it in water.
5. Abrade it with a coin or a knife.

How these procedures correlate with those of ASTM or Federal Specifications test methods or those of other standards making bodies is yet to be determined.

Manufacturers Literature

We come now to an assessment of the manufacturers literature. How valid is such literature? What input has the manufacturer made in assembling the information that goes into a piece of literature? How does the manufacturer determine what tests are to be performed? Was a rational approach used to determine what tests should be performed on this new product. Generally the manufacturer tests for what they think is pertinent, but they rarely use a prescribed methodology. Many manufacturers overlook, or are unaware of, the interaction of their product with adjacent products when they determine what kind of tests to run on their product and what kind of information to show in their literature. There is a whole host of information that a manufacturer has neglected to inform himself about simply because he is not knowledgeable about building construction. These are areas that only a design professional can appreciate and understand in dealing with several materials coming into contact with one another.

The user, therefore, cannot rely solely on the manufacturers claims and statements. If the reports are valid and if other tests, perhaps more pertinent for the intended use of the product, should be performed, it must be determined by the design professional.

Selection Responsibilities

It is becoming more essential to create a more meaningful and rational approach to materials evaluation. The most apparent reason is the need to avoid errors and omissions; this is evident because of the increasing number of suits brought by building owners against architects and contractors for utilizing and selecting products or systems that have failed. These failures can occur because of an incorrect application, a wrong mating of contiguous materials resulting in an incompatibility, or an incorrect evaluation resulting in a poor selection for the intended use.

The design professional (specifier, architect, engineer) has a responsibility for having an adequate knowledge of the science of design and construction. By virtue of the state licensing laws, the design professional impliedly represents that reasonable care, judgment, and technical skill in selecting, specifying, using, and approving materials, products, equipment, and systems will be exercised.

The Need for Effective Product Evaluation

There are a number of compelling reasons that motivate the design professional to exercise care in the evaluation and selection process. In recent years consumers and building owners have become more aware and informed and increasingly design professionals are being held accountable for errors and omissions that may be committed in the inappropriate selection of materials and products. Also it is less expensive to generate repeat business from existing clients than it is to cultivate and seek new clients. By keeping errors and omissions to a minimum the design professional will retain satisfied clients. In some instances the inadequate or hastily concluded evaluation process may result in some grievous harm or fatal injury that may lead to ugly litigation in the courts that is not a boon to anyone's professional standing.

HAROLD J. ROSEN
PHILIP M. BENNETT

Merrick, New York
Madison, Wisconsin
July, 1979

Contents

Part 1 A Recommended Approach to Evaluation and Selection

Harold J. Rosen

1.1 A Structured Approach to Materials Evaluation
and Selection   3
1.2 Working with the System   24
1.3 Contractor Involvement   45

Part 2 Developing the Systematic Approach

Philip M. Bennett

2.1 The Need   53
2.2 The Systematic Approach   63
2.3 System Development   75
2.4 Responsibilities of the Design Professional   98
2.5 Use of a Systematic Approach   107

Glossary   131

References   133

APPENDIX Building, Housing, and Allied Research
Centers Throughout the World   135

INDEX   159

PART ONE

A Recommended Approach to Evaluation and Selection

HAROLD J. ROSEN

1.1 A Structured Approach to Materials Evaluation and Selection, 3
Introduction, 3
Materials Evaluation and Selection, 4
Establishing Workable Tools, 4

Chart 1   Hud Operation Breakthrough, 5
Chart 2   PBS Performance Specifications for Office Buildings, 6
Chart 3   A Master List of Properties for Building Materials and
            Products, 7

Refining the Evaluation and Selection Process, 16
Highlights of the Major Performance Requirements, 17
Expanding the Performance Requirements, 18

Chart 4   Checklist of Performance Requirements, 19

Research Organizations, 23

2   A Recommended Approach to Evaluation and Selection

1.2   Working with the System, 24
Essentials of the Performance Concept, 24
Evaluating a New Product, 24
Selecting a Product for a New Project, 25

Chart   5   Evaluation Techniques, 26
Chart   6   Selection Technique, 27

Test Method References, 27

Chart   7   Test Methods for Coatings, 28
Chart   8   Test Methods for Insulation, 29
Chart   9   Test Methods for Plastics, 30
Chart 10   Test Methods for Rubber Materials, 31

A Case Study, 32

Chart 11   Evaluation of Siporex as an Exterior Wall, 33
Chart 12   Test Methods Cited in Chart 11, 39

Judgment, Simulation, Experience, 39

Chart 13   Cross Section of Structure, 40

Summary, 44

1.3   Contractor Involvement, 45

Chart 14   Field Check List for Elastomeric Sealants 07900, 46

1.1

A Structured Approach to Materials
Evaluation and Selection

Introduction

To achieve a more successful solution to our current haphazard, un-
scientific approach to materials evaluation and selection, it is essential
to structure a meaningful methodology that can be employed by the
user. Obviously it requires more proficient materials technologists who
have a more complete understanding of basic materials. The complexity of today's materials generated by the products of chemistry and
metallurgy are beyond the range of most architects and contractors.

The evaluation of materials by means of a standardized organized
approach has not been formulated by any of the organizations involved in design or construction. Neither is there any governmental
agency or independent board that evaluates materials by means of
some adopted standards. When we use the term "material," other
terms such as product, equipment, component, subsystem, system, and
assembly can be substituted for the word "material," since the evaluation and selection process used to assess a "material" can likewise be
applied to the ascending categories of more complex situations.

3

Materials Evaluation and Selection

Materials evaluation and selection is really concerned with two major areas: (1) the evaluation of a new material and (2) the evaluation and selection of materials for use in a new project.

New materials can actually be separated into two distinct categories: (a) those that are manufactured to meet an existing standard and (b) those that are unique in that no standard exists against which they can be measured and therefore require an investigation and assessment as to the claims of the manufacturer. New materials that fall into the first category are readily evaluated against a product standard. Good product standards are the result of systematic technical research efforts combined with committee work such as ASTM, Federal Specifications, and ANSI standards. These standards establish suitable physical and/or chemical properties that for the most part have a direct relation to performance. Through use these standards are upgraded as additional knowledge of a product's performance is obtained from the field. New products that are claimed by the manufacturer as meeting a product standard can therefore be quite readily evaluated against the product standard.

Establishing Workable Tools

New products marketed without reference to a product standard require a completely different evaluation approach. There is, however, a basic tool that can be utilized to establish a rational methodology for the investigation and evaluation of materials, products, and systems for which there are no known standards. This tool is the performance concept.

Another tool employed in this structured approach is a checklist that codifies all performance requirements by major divisions so that a workable matrix is established. To illustrate this approach one can envision the CSI Format. Rather than listing hundreds of section titles either alphabetically or numerically, they are grouped by a trades

CHART 1. Hud Operation Breakthrough

			Attributes								
Built elements			Structural serviceability	Structural safety	Health and safety	Fire safety	Acoustic environment	Illuminated environment	Atmospheric environment	Durability/time reliability (function)	Spatial characteristics and arrangement
			1	2	3	4	5	6	7	8	9
Structure		A									
Interior space dividers	Walls and doors, inter—dwelling	B									
	Walls and doors, intra—dwelling	C									
	Floor—ceiling	D									
Exterior envelope	Walls, doors and windows	E									
	Roof—ceiling, ground floor	F									
Fixtures and hardware		G									
Plumbing		H									
Mechanical equipment, appliances		I									
Power, electrical distribution, communications		J									
Lighting elements		K									
Enclosed spaces		L									

relationship under 16 major divisions. Such an approach enables the user to quickly ascertain the location of any item used in building construction with respect to specification sections, manufacturer's literature, and cost estimating.

Two early examples of a performance approach to building construction are also illustrated. Chart 1 shows a matrix utilized in "Operation Breakthrough" by the U. S. Department of Housing and Urban Development and Chart 2 by the U. S. General Services Administration. In both illustrations the matrices identify "Attributes," which in

CHART 2.   PBS Performance Specifications for Office Buildings

Built elements or subsystems

Attributes		1 Structure	2 HVAC	3 Electrical distribution	4 Luminaires	5 Finished floor	6 Finished ceiling	7 Space dividers
a	Conditioned air							
b	Illumination							
c	Acoustics							
d	Stability durability							
e	Health and safety							
f	Maintenance							
g	Planning							

essence are performance requirements, and the "Built Elements," which are to be investigated for the specific "attribute" or performance requirement. However, in both illustrations the "attributes" or performance requirements are limited and the "built elements" to be investigated are limited.

If we look at Chart 3, our approach will appear analagous to the CSI Format, namely a listing of major divisons for materials and products with specific properties outlined under each division.

CHART 3. A Master List of Properties for Building Materials and Products by the International Council for Building Research, Studies, and Documentation

1 PROPERTIES

1.1 General Information

Description, sufficient to indicate type of material or product and its use; classification symbol (e.g., clay bricks).

Trade name or brand; type or quality

Identification of standards and norms, giving country of origin. If standards do not exist, statement of quality according to some other recognized authority; quality control; quality mark.

General statement on the purpose and use of the product (see also section 2 where a more detailed description of the use of the product is given in special cases)

Accessories

1.2 Composition, Method of Manufacture

Composition

Manufacture and construction; Structure, external, particularly for built-up products or prefabricated building elements; Method of preparation, manufacture and finish, including, e.g., impregnation, coating, grinding, polishing, etc.

1.3 Shape, Dimensions, Weight

Shape (when possible, include a drawing or isometric sketch)

Dimensions. Production tolerances for dimensions and shape; principle for coordination of dimensions with other building elements; need of space; sieve analysis; specific surface

Geometric properties of section (moment of inertia, modulus of section, etc.)

Volume

Weight

1.4   General Appearance

Character of visible face and arrises (also edges and corners)

Evenness, physical smoothness, and flatness of surface

Appearance of visible face; texture, grain, colour, embossing or relief pattern, etc.

Transparency; translucency (See also section 1.5, optical properties)

1.5   Physical, Chemical and Biological Properties

Physical, chemical, and biological properties of the material or product determined by testing the material, component or building unit

Specific weight; bulk density; weight per unit volume

Internal structure; porosity

Chemical analysis

Permeability to air and gases (water vapor, see permeability to water vapor diffusion)

Properties relating to the presence of water

Moisture content

Solubility in water

Capillarity

Water absorption

Permeability to water and other liquids under the influence of pressure; resistance to hydrostatic water pressure

Permeability to water vapor diffusion

Drying; evaporation

Moisture expansion and drying shrinkage; dimensional changes with changes in moisture content (setting shrinkage and expansion, see change in volume due to chemical reactions)

Thermal properties

Thermal movements; linear expansion

Specific heat

Freezing point, melting point, boiling point

Radiation coefficient

Thermal conductivity; air-to-air transmission coefficient

Warmth to touch

Effect of high and low temperatures

Effect of changes in temperature (e.g., thermal shock, effect of frost)

Strength properties

Properties in tension

Properties in compression

Properties in shear

Properties in bending

Properties in torsion

Impact strength

Hardness

Resistance to fatigue

Mechanical properties

Resistance to mechanical wear

Resistance to insertion and extraction of nails and screws

Resistance to splitting

Resistance to tearing

Resistance to bursting

Rheological properties, e.g., viscosity, plasticity (flow, plastic, creep, etc.)

Frictional resistance

Coefficient of friction

Degree of slipperiness in use

Adhesion (bond strength) under tension or shearing

Acoustic properties

Sound absorption, sound reflection

CHART 3.   A Master List of Properties for Building Materials and
Products by the International Council for Building Research, Studies,
and Documentation (Continued)

Sound transmission

Optical properties

Light absorption; light reflection; specular and diffusing reflection; brilliancy

Light transmission; specular and diffusing transmission

Light refraction; refractive index; light dispersion

Optical distortion

Electrical and magnetic properties

Electrical conductivity (or resistance)

Dielectric constant

Liability to develop and shed electrostatic charges

Effect of sunlight

Radiation properties (emission, protection)

Effect of frost

Effect of fire

Combustibility including flash point, production of gases and fumes when burnt, liability for self-ignition

Fire resistance (see also section 1.9)

Surface spread of flame

Effect of chemicals (including water); also corroding agents

Effect of impurities

Effect of and protection against microorganisms, mildew fungus, insects vermin, etc.

Reaction with other materials (e.g., aggressiveness, protection)

Changes in behavior during preparation and subsequent use

Setting time

Heat evolution

Change in volume due to chemical reactions (e.g., setting shrinkage), (see section 1.8, drying time)

Properties important from the point of view of hygiene, comfort, and safety

Toxicity

Emission of odors

Taintability

Tendency to deposit dust, etc.

Tendency to injure the skin, respiratory organs, etc.

Liability to vermin infestation, etc.

Liability to become dirty; ease of cleaning

Safety

1.6 Durability

Although no specific headings can be given here, information must be provided even if only in general terms

Notes. a Durability factors that affect design considerations are dealt with in section 3. Special maintenance requirements are dealt with in section 3.3

b Because the changes in properties affecting durability depend upon time, exposure, and usage conditions and the amount of maintenance carried out, the information cannot normally be obtained from laboratory tests only but must also be derived from experience, including field investigations. This will often lead to an assessment rather than to a statement

c Avoid very general assessments such as "durability very good," etc.

d In view of the complexity of the assessments, the information given should include brief details of the basis of each assessment

e When the durability depends upon the degree of exposure of the material, the position of the material or component in a building may be critical and if so it should be taken into account in making the assessment

Examples. Some materials become brittle in the course of time but this may not affect their life when placed in those parts of a building where they are not subject to impact

11

CHART 3.   A Master List of Properties for Building Materials and
Products by the International Council for Building Research, Studies,
and Documentation (Continued)

1.7   Special Technical Properties for Installation, Mechanical Plant, Equipment, etc.

Notes.   a The properties of the constructional elements of the apparatus, etc., are given, when required, under section 1.5

b Under section 1.9 are given properties of the functional elements of the building to meet functional requirements

Method of operation

Connection data

Data for "mechanical" connection, to a working medium, e.g., compressed air, water, steam, etc., dimensions of connection

Data on connection to source of energy

Performance data

Simple mechanical data, e.g., power, moment, effect, speed

Capacity

Other performance data, e.g., temperature

Consumption of energy and ancillary materials

Supplied energy

Consumption of ancillary materials, e.g., lubrication oil, etc.

Efficiency

Maneuverability and control

Other technical data in normal condition

Mechanical

Thermal

Electric

Secondary effects and disturbances during operation (noise, vibrations, etc.)

1.8   Working Characteristics

Technical properties of special interest in processing, handling and transport

Note.   Since these properties are important to large groups of people in the building trade, they have been collected in this separate section. References should be made, as required, to other parts of the schedule.

Ease of handling

Consistence; workability; working time

Ease of sawing, cutting, boring, punching, bending, etc.; work hardening (also the influence on the cut by the tool and on the tool)

Capability to be welded; capability to be jointed to itself or other materials by adhesives; suitable adhesives and their properties

Properties of importance in connection with fixing; means of fixing the product (nailability, ease of extraction of nails and screws)

Surface treatments: relevant properties

Suitability of the material to receive a surface treatment

Spreadability. Coverage. Hiding power

Drying time, etc.

Ability to withstand rough handling and transport (shaking, crushing, compression, etc.)

Ability to withstand storage

1.9 Functional Properties of Common Types of Building Elements in which the Material or Product is Incorporated

Note. The data refer to correctly built constructional work in accordance with the considerations for design and building in sections 2 and 3.

Strength and stability (static and dynamic loading)

Fire resistance (classification according to fire resistance)

Protection against water, moisture, and moisture movements (expansion and shrinkage)

Protection against rainfall, ground water

Protection against water vapor

Protection against cold and heat; thermal insulation

Protection against wind, gases, etc.

Protection against sound; sound insulation and sound absorption

Protection against radiation

13

CHART 3.   A Master List of Properties for Building Materials and
Products by the International Council for Building Research, Studies,
and Documentation (Continued)

Special protection against other agencies, e.g., protection against impurity, protection against dust, protection against burglary, etc.

Durability

General functional behavior

2   DESIGN CONSIDERATIONS AND DETAILS. SUITABLE APPLICATIONS

2.1   Considerations for Design and Building: Suitable Applications

The proper use of the material or the product in the building in order that the latter meets functional requirements and relevant regulations. Limitations in use (a subdivision could be made similar to that of section 1.9)

Need of special units, accessories and fittings

The effect of the material or product on adjacent constructional materials and vice versa

Interchangeability; repairability; replaceability

2.2   Architectural and Constructional Details

2.3   Examples of Common Mistakes in Design and Work

2.4   References to Finished Constructions. Case Studies

3   INSTRUCTIONS FOR WORK AND MAINTENANCE

3.1   Working Instructions

Method of construction and of working, type of labor, erection, handling

Special plant or tools and other special arrangements for work on the site and maintenance, including safety to operatives

Preparatory work off the site

Transport to and on the building site

Storage on the site. Precautions required for storage on site

CHART 3.   A Master List of Properties for Building Materials and
Products by the International Council for Building Research, Studies,
and Documentation (Continued)

Preparatory work on the site (e.g., mixing, measuring, scaffolding, etc.) Need for temporary supports

Protection against adjacent work

Protection of adjacent work

Protection against weather

Erection and work on the site (e.g., method of jointing)

Surface treatment; method of finishing (external and internal), including touching up; adjusting

Cleaning up

Waste reduction

3.2   Site Testing

3.3   Instructions for Cleaning and Maintenance

Cleaning

Maintenance method and frequency

Repair and replacement; need for specialist repairers

4   ECONOMICS

4.1   Materials consumption and normal wastage

4.2   Rates of erection, fixing, etc.

4.3   Specifications of prices and costs (these refer to materials, building elements, finished constructions and maintenance); details of freight, etc.

5   SPECIFICATION OF DISTRIBUTION

5.1   Production and supply capacity

5.2   Packing

5.3   Conditions of delivery

CHART 3.   A Master List of Properties for Building Materials and
Products by the International Council for Building Research, Studies,
and Documentation (Continued)

5.4   Guarantees

5.5   Directions when ordering

6   SALES ORGANIZATION. CONTRACT WORK. TECHNICAL
     SERVICE

    6.1   Sales and contract organization

    6.2   Technical and commercial advice

    6.3   References to trade catalogues, detail drawings, etc.

7   REFERENCES TO LITERATURE

Refining The Evaluation and Selection Process

As we examine the concept of performance and the illustrations shown
in Charts 1, 2, and 3, we recognize that a structured approach to
materials evaluation and selection can be achieved based on these
principles with a more refined matrix.

    The system for rational evaluation consists of two basic ingredients:
(1) a checklist consisting of several broad qualitative headings or performance requirements that are then expanded to a series of
subordinate characteristics and (2) a method of assessing and measuring the performance characteristics or criteria. A matrix can then be
prepared that permits the user to subject any new material to comprehensive investigation and evaluation. The checklist's broad qualitative
headings can be reduced to nine major performance requirements, "attributes" as follows:

1. Structural serviceability.
2. Fire safety.

3. Habitability.
4. Durability.
5. Practicability.
6. Compatibility.
7. Maintainability.
8. Code acceptability.
9. Economics.

Highlights of the Major Performance Requirements

To understand each of these major performance requirements or "attributes" the following generalizations can be made for each category.

1. *Structural Serviceability.* Includes resistance to natural forces such as wind and earthquake; structural adequacy and physical properties such as strength, compression, tensile forces, shear, and behavior against impact and indentation.

Note: For specific "materials" where structural serviceability is not a factor, the investigation into this performance requirement is not applicable.

2. *Fire Safety.* Includes resistance against the effects of fire such as flame propogation, burn through, smoke, toxic gases, etc.

3. *Habitability.* Includes livability relative to thermal efficiency, acoustic properties, water permeability, optical properties, hygiene, comfort, light and ventilation, etc.

4. *Durability.* Includes ability to withstand wear, weather resistance such as ozone and UV, dimensional stability, etc.

5. *Practicability.* Ability to surmount field conditions such as transportation, storage, handling, tolerances, connections, site hazards, etc.

Note: Transportation of huge prefabricated elements will require investigation with respect to roads, bridges, and tunnels to assure passage. Investigation of tolerances of dissimilar elements such as a concrete frame or a structural steel frame to receive precast concrete or metal and glass curtain walls.

6. *Compatability.* Ability to withstand reaction with adjacent materials in terms of chemical interaction, galvanic action, ability to be coated, etc.

Note: In using a sealant will it stain adjacent surfaces, will there be any chemical interaction with other backup materials?

7. *Maintainability.* Ease of cleaning, repairability of punctures, gouges and tears, recoating etc.

Note: For factory baked-on paint finishes, are there any satisfactory retouching materials to cover scratches or other minor defects resulting from installation or use?

8. *Code Acceptability.* Includes review of code and manufacture's claims as to code compliance.
9. *Economics.* Includes installed costs, maintenance costs, budgetary limitations.

Expanding The Performance Requirements

The performance requirements or "attributes" listed above can now be expanded to list more specific performance requirements that although it may not be all inclusive, will serve as a guide to the user and should stimulate consideration of additional performance requirements when utilizing the matrix shown as Chart 4.

CHART 4. Checklist of Performance Requirements

1 **STRUCTURAL SERVICEABILITY**

    1.1 Natural forces

        1.1.1 Wind

        1.1.2 Seismic

    1.2 Strength Properties

        1.2.1 Compression

        1.2.2 Tension

        1.2.3 Shear

        1.2.4 Torsion

        1.2.5 Modulus of Rupture

        1.2.6 Impact

        1.2.7 Indentation

        1.2.8 Hardness

2 **FIRE SAFETY**

    2.1 Fire resistance

    2.2 Flame spread

    2.3 Smoke development

    2.4 Toxicity

    2.5 Fuel load

    2.6 Combustibility

3 **HABITABILITY**

    3.1 Thermal properties

        3.1.1 Thermal conductivity

        3.1.2 Thermal expansion

        3.1.3 Thermal shock

    3.2 Acoustic properties

        3.2.1 Sound transmission

        3.2.2 Sound absorption

        3.2.3 Sound reverberation

    3.3 Water permeability

        3.3.1 Water absorption

CHART 4. Checklist of Performance Requirements (Continued)

3.3.2   Permeability

3.3.3   Water vapor transmission

3.3.4   Moisture expansion and drying shrinkage

3.3.5   Water infiltration

3.4   Optical properties

    3.4.1   Light transmission

    3.4.2   Light absorption

    3.4.3   Light refraction

    3.4.4   Optical distortion

3.5   Hygiene, comfort, safety

    3.5.1   Toxicity

    3.5.2   Emission of odors

    3.5.3   Vermin infestation

    3.5.4   Slip resistance

    3.5.5   Mildew resistance

    3.5.6   Air infiltration

4   DURABILITY

4.1   Resistance to wear

    4.1.1   Abrasion resistance

    4.1.2   Scratch resistance

4.2   Weathering

    4.2.1   Freeze-thaw

    4.2.2   Ozone

    4.2.3   Fading

    4.2.4   Chemical fumes

    4.2.5   Bactericidal

    4.2.6   Ultraviolet radiation

4.3   Adhesion of coatings

    4.3.1   Delamination

    4.3.2   Blistering

4.4   Dimensional stability

    4.4.1   Shrinkage

    4.4.2   Expansion

CHART 4.   Checklist of Performance Requirements (Continued)

    4.4.3   Volume change

4.5   Mechanical properties

    4.5.1   Resistance to splitting

    4.5.2   Resistance to bursting

    4.5.3   Resistance to tearing

    4.5.4   Resistance to fatigue

4.6   Rheological properties

    4.6.1   Viscosity

    4.6.2   Plasticity

5   PRACTICABILITY

2 5.1   Transport

    5.1.1   Limitations with respect to size, weight, handling

5.2   Storage on site

    5.2.1   Protection against elements

5.3   Handling during installation

    5.3.1   Abrasion

    5.3.2   Breakage

    5.3.3   Patching

5.4   Field tolerances

    5.4.1   Corrective measures

5.5   Connections

    5.5.1   Resistance to insertion and extraction of fasteners

6   COMPATABILITY

6.1   Jointing materials

    6.1.1   Adherence of sealants

    6.1.2   Staining of sealants

6.2   Coatings

    6.2.1   Ability to receive and retain coatings

6.3   Galvanic Interaction or Corrosion Resistance

    6.3.1   Steel

    6.3.2   Aluminum

    6.3.3   Wood

CHART 4.   Checklist of Performance Requirements (Continued)

6.3.4   Stainless steel
6.3.5   Copper, brass, or bronze

7   MAINTAINABILITY

7.1   Compatibility of coatings
    7.1.1   Interaction
    7.1.2   Delamination
    7.1.3   Blistering
7.2   Indentation and puncture
    7.2.1   Patching
7.3   Chemical or graffitti attack
    7.3.1   Cleanability
    7.3.2   Resistance to attack

8   CODE ACCEPTABILITY

8.1   Review of Code
    8.1.1   Compliance

9   ECONOMICS

9.1   Installed costs
9.2   Maintenance Costs

The nine major performance requirements or "attributes" of the checklist and their listed criteria can be expanded as needed to investigate specific products, equipment, or systems. For each requirement in turn we can establish criteria and test methods to check findings. Thus, this tool can be used to develop new products by setting forth performance requirements and working with manufacturers to assure realistic criteria. It is a tool that can upgrade existing products too. Manufacturers may find it helpful in verifying and completing new and old product data sheets. A review of framework parameters can assure that significant requirements have been investigated and set forth.

Ideally the system will work best when the design professional is a materials technologist with broad perspective on materials. However, professionals with lesser proficiency in materials will benefit as well. They will have a structured framework with comprehensive information on criteria and test methods. To make an intelligent evaluation or selection of materials and products the specifier will turn increasingly to this or a comparable rational method for analysis and assessment.

Research Organizations

General research and highly specialized research into building products and systems are conducted by both private organizations and governmental research centers throughout the world. Informational bulletins, papers, and standards based on this research are oftentimes available from these sources. A listing of these sources compiled and included in Overseas Building Note No. 163, by the Building Research Establishment, Garston, Watford WD2 7JR, England is included in the Appendix. Information gleaned from these sources is very valuable in evaluating and selecting products, especially when a project is being designed for a climate and a location that imposes peculiar characteristics. Revised current lists of the Appendix may be obtained from the Building Research Establishment.

1.2

Working with the System

Essentials of the Performance Concept

For many of the performance requirements listed in Chart 4, the performance concept can be utilized to measure the performance characteristics. For some of the performance requirements, notably practicability, the method of assessment is one of judgement, simulation and/or experience.

The performance concept is developed on the basis of three major categories: requirement, criterion, and test as follows:

Requirement.   A qualitative statement of the desired performance.

Criteria.   A quantitative statement of the desired performance.

Test.   An evaluative procedure to assure compliance with the Criteria.

Evaluating A New Product

To illustrate a simple procedure in evaluating a new product, the user would review the manufacturer's product literature with the checklist as shown in Chart 4. If information on fire safety was missing in the

24

product literature the user would request information from the manufacturer as follows:

Requirement.   Furnish fire safety information on your acoustical product-brand "X."

Criterion.   Flame Spread Index.

Test.   ASTM E84.

Result.   ?

Similarly for any other performance requirement designated in Chart 4 that the user determines to be appropriate but is not included in the manufacturer's data sheet, the user would determine the requirement, criterion, and test method to be used so that the manufacturer could test the specific attribute and furnish the test result. If a standard test method is not in existence, the user might require some simulated test to check a specific requirement.

In evaluating a new material, product, or system, the user is simply checking to determine whether the manufacturer has provided all the essential data that the user may require or believe is essential. He will then look at the test results to determine whether the new product possesses certain characteristics that are not available in other products, or he can design around certain limitations that the new product has.

Selecting a Product for a New Project

The system can also be used to establish requirements for the selection of products, materials, or systems for a new project. In this instance the user in addition to setting forth performance requirements, criteria, and test methods, establishes what he considers to be the necessary performance levels, for an acoustical tile as follows:

Requirement	Criterion	Test	Result
Fire Safety	Flame Spread	ASTM E84	Less than 25
Habitability	Light Reflectance	ASTM C523	More than 0.75

To reiterate, in evaluating a new "material" follow procedure outlined in Chart 5; to select a "material" for a new project follow procedure outlined in Chart 6.

CHART 5. Evaluation Technique

1 MATERIAL

2 PRODUCT

3 EQUIPMENT

4 COMPONENT

5 SYSTEM

   A Review manufacturer's literature.

   B Review checklist performance requirements.

   C List Missing Criteria.

   D Ask Manufacturer to obtain test results for missing criteria.

Example. Product literature for acoustical tile does not contain data for water absorption. Establish test method and request results.

Criteria	Test Method	Result
Water absorption	ASTM	
Shrinkage		
Expansion		

CHART 6.   Selection Technique

1   MATERIAL
2   PRODUCT
3   EQUIPMENT
4   COMPONENT
5   SYSTEM

A   Review requirements of building item for its location in the project.
B   Review parameters of usage.
C   Establish criteria, test methods and results expected.

Example.   Acoustical tile for wet area.

Criteria	Test Method	Result
Water absorption	ASTM	None or negligible
Dimensional stability	Fed. Spec.	
Shrinkage		None
Expansion		None

Test Method References

The user frequently requires standard test method references for use in the evaluation and selection process. ASTM and Federal Specification Test Methods are both good sources to utilize in this assessment. Charts 7 to 10 are compilations of various test methods for coatings, insulation, plastics, and rubber materials.

CHART 7. Test Methods for Coatings

Type of Test	Test Designation
Abrasion, resistance to	ASTM D658, D968, Fed. Std. 141a
Adhesion	ASTM B571, C633, D2197, D3359, ISO 2819
Atmospheric pollutants, resistance to	ASTM B117, B287, D1543, D1654, D3129, G1, G33, Fed. Std. 141a, Fed. Specs. TT-P-31D, TT-P-103B, TT-C-530A, TT-C-00498A, TT-E-516A, TT-E-522A, TT-P-102D
Cleanability	ASTM C756, D2486
Color change	ASTM D1535, D1543, D1729, D2244, D2616, G45
Corrosion resistance	ASTM B117, D1014, D1654, D2933, G1, ISO 1462
Flammability	ASTM D1360, E162, E286
Flexural strength	ASTM B571, D522, D1737, Fed. Std. 141a
Fungus resistance	ASTM D3129, D3272, D3273, G21, Mil. Std. 810C, Fed. Std. 141a, Fed. Specs. TT-P-31D, TT-P-51D, TT-P-61E, TT-P-71E, TT-P-81E, TT-P-19C, TT-P-55B
Gloss	ASTM D523, D1471
Impact resistance	ASTM D1474, D2794, D3170, SAE J400
Moisture, resistance to	ASTM D1010, D1187, D1735, D2246, D2247, D2366, D2932, Mil. Std. 810C, Fed. Specs. TT-P-641F, TT-C-1079A
Optical properties	ASTM E97, E424, E434
Permeability	ASTM C355, D1653, E96
Physical integrity	
checking	ASTM D660
cracking	ASTM D661
Scratch resistance	ASTM D2197
Surface uniformity	ASTM C536
Tensile strength	ASTM D522, D1737, D2370
Thermal aging, resistance to	ASTM D2246, Mil. Std. 810C

CHART 7. Test Methods for Coatings (Continued)

Thickness	ASTM B567, D1005, D1186, D1400, E376, ISO 2178, 2360, 2361
Weathering, resistance to	ASTM D822, D1006, D1014, D2620, G7, G23, G24, G25, G26, G27, Mil. Std. 810C, Fed. Std. 141a, Fed. Specs. TT-P-31D, TT-P-61E, TT-P-71E, TT-P-81E, TT-C-530A, TT-P-19C, TT-P-55B, TT-P-95B, TT-P-1181A, TT-C-00498A, TT-E-516A, TT-E-522A, TT-P-37C, TT-P-102D

CHART 8. Test Methods for Insulation

Type of Test	Test Designation
Atmospheric pollutants, resistance to ·	
Biodeterioration	ASTM D3273, G21, G22
Breaking strength	ASTM C446
Compressive strength	ASTM C165
Deflection	ASTM C209
Density	ASTM C167, C209, C302, C303, C519, C520
Dimensional stability	ASTM C548, D1042
Expansion	ASTM D1037
Flame spread	ASTM E84
Flexural strength	ASTM C203
Impact resistance (by dropping)	ASTM C487
Indentation hardness	ASTM C569
Mechanical stability	ASTM C421
Moisture absorption	ASTM C209
Moisture, resistance to	Mil. Std. 810C
Parting strength	ASTM C686
Properties at abnormal temperature	ASTM D759
Racking load	ASTM E72
Specific heat	ASTM C351
Tensile strength	ASTM C209
Thermal aging, resistance to	ASTM C356, C411, C447, D794, Mil. Std. 810C

29

CHART 8. Test Methods for Insulation (Continued)

Thermal conductivity	ASTM C177, C236, C335, C518, C745, D2326
Thermal resistance	ASTM C653, C687
Thermal transference	ASTM C691
Thickness	ASTM C167, C209
Transverse strength	ASTM C209
Vapor permeability	ASTM C355, E96
Weathering, resistance to	ASTM G7

CHART 9. Test Methods for Plastics

Type of Test	Test Designation
Abrasion, mar, resistance to	ASTM D673, D1044, D1242
Atmospheric pollutants, resistance to	ASTM B117, B287, D543, D1149, D1712, G1, G33, Fed. Std. 406
Blister-delamination	ASTM C363
Burst strength	ASTM D774
Cleanability	AIMA-7
Coefficient of expansion	ASTM D696, D864, D1204
Color change	ASTM D1729, D1925, D2244, D2616, D3134, G45, Fed. Std. 141
Creep	ASTM D674, D2552, D2648, D2990, D2991, Fed. Std. 406
Deflection	ASTM D621, D648
Density	ASTM D792, D1505
Embrittlement	ASTM D1790
Fatigue	ASTM C394, D671, SAE J783
Flammability	ASTM D635, D1692, D1929, D3014, E84, E136
Flatness	ASTM D1604, Fed. Spec. DD-G-1403, Mil. Spce. 3787
Flexural strength	ASTM C393, D747, D790
Fungus resistance	ASTM G21, G22, G29, Fed. Std. 406, Fed. Spec. L-P-380C
Impact strength	ASTM D256, D1790, D1822, D3029, D3099, D3420, ANSI Z97.1, Fed. Std. 406

30

CHART 9. Test Methods for Plastics (Continued)

Indentation-hardness	ASTM D785, D2240, D2583, Fed. Std. 406
Modulus of elasticity	ASTM D638, D695, D882
Moisture, resistance to	ASTM D756, D2126, D2383, Mil. Std. 810C, Fed. Spec. L-P-380C
Optical properties	ASTM E424, E434, Fed. Spec. DD-G-451
Permeability	ASTM C355, D1434, E96, F372, Fed. Std. 406, TAPPI T-482
Refractive index	ASTM D542
Scratches, defects	Fed. Spec. DD-G-1403
Tensile strength	ASTM C297, D638, D882
Thermal aging, resistance to	ASTM D648, D793, D1299, D2115, D2126, D2288, D2445, D2951, D3045, Mil. Std. 810C
Thermal conductivity	ASTM C177, C518, D2326
Thickness	ASTM D374, D1777
Ultimate elongation	ASTM D638, D882
Warping, bowing	ASTM D709, D1181
Weathering, resistance to	ASTM D1435, D1499, D1501, D2565, G7, G23, G24, G25, G26, G27, Fed. Spec. L-P-508f, Fed. Std. 406, ANSI Z97.1
Wind, resistance to	ASTM E330

CHART 10. Test Methods for Rubber Materials

Type of Test	Test Designation
Adhesion/cohesion	ASTM C719, C766
Adhesion, peel	ASTM C794, D413, D429, D903, D1781, D1876, D2630
Atmospheric pollutants, resistance to	ASTM D518, D1149 (ozone)
Brittleness point	ASTM D2137
Compression-recovery	ASTM F36
Compression set	ASTM D395, D1229
Creep resistance	ASTM D1390, D1456, D1780, D2293, D2294, F38
Extrusion rate	ASTM C603

31

CHART 10. Test Methods for Rubber Materials (Continued)

Flexural strength	ASTM D1184
Flow properties	ASTM C639
Fungus resistance	ASTM D1286, D1877
Impact strength	ASTM D950
Hardness	ASTM C661, D1415, D2240
Low temperature flexibility	ASTM C711, C734, C765, D797, D1053, D1329, D2137
Moisture or liquid immersion, resistance to	ASTM D471, D1101, D1151, D1460, D3137, F82
Sealability	ASTM D1081, F37, F112
Shear strength	ASTM D905, D1002, D2919, D3165
Staining	ASTM D925, D2203
Tear resistance	ASTM D624
Tensile strength	ASTM D412, D897, D906, D2095, D2295, F152
Thermal aging, resistance to	ASTM C771, C792, D573, D865, D1870
Ultimate elongation	ASTM D412
Weathering, resistance to	ASTM C718, C732, C793, D904, D1171, D1183, D1828, D2559, ANSI A116.1, AAMA 802.2, 804.1, 805.2, 806.1, 807.1, 808.1, Fed. Specs. TT-G-410E, TT-S-00227E, TT-S-00230C, TT-S-001543A, TT-S-001657
Young's modulus	ASTM D797

A Case Study

A more comprehensive materials investigation was performed by the author on a European product called "Siporex," which is a lightweight concrete used for blocks and planking. With only a minimum of information contained in the product literature, the following evaluation chart was prepared (Chart 11) to solicit additional information from the manufacturer to establish its potentials and limitations. The test methods cited in Chart 11 are amplified in Chart 12.

CHART 11.   Evaluation of Siporex as an Exterior Wall

Requirement		Criterion	Test Method	Result
1.	Structural Stability	1.1 Impact resistance	ASTM E–72, Section 13	
		1.2 Modulus of rupture	ASTM C683	
		1.3 Support for attached loads	Bookshelf at 40 lb/lin. ft	
		1.4 Wind resistance	Apply 50 lb/sq. ft for 1 min and report damage	
		1.5 Compressive load	ASTM E–72, Section 7	
		1.6 Pull-out resistance	Analysis or physical simulation	
		1.7 Seismic resistance	Analysis or computation	
		1.8 Cut-out for service elements—mechanical electrical	Analysis or physical simulation	
		1.9 Puncture resistance		
		1.10 Resistance to point impact	Fed. Test Method Std. 406, Method 1074.	
2.	Fire Safety	2.1 Fire endurance	ASTM E19	8 in. block–4 hrs.
		2.2 Flame spread	ASTM E84	
		2.3 Smoke developed	ASTM E84	
		2.4 Toxicity	Animal inhalation test	

CHART 11. Evaluation of Siporex as an Exterior Wall (Continued)

Requirement		Criterion	Test Method	Result
3. Habitability	3.1	Thermal Properties		
		3.1.1 Thermal conductivity	"K" factor ASTM C177	0.81
		3.1.2 Thermal expansion	ASTM E228	4.5×10^{-6}
		3.1.3 Thermal shock	Rapid heating and cooling	
	3.2	Acoustic Properties		
		3.2.1 Sound transmission	ASTM E90	
		3.2.2 Sound reverberation	ASTM C423	
		3.2.3 Sound absorption	ASTM C423	
	3.3	Water Permeability		
		3.3.1 Water absorption	ASTM C140	
		3.3.2 Permeability	Fed. Spec. TT-P-0035 (E514)	
		3.3.3 Water vapor transmission	ASTM C355	
		3.3.4 Moisture Expansion and Drying shrinkage	ASTM C426	0.07

Note: Since the material will take on water it is essential to protect elements from condensed moisture that could impair structural adequacy through deterioration. Provide adequate vapor barriers, ventilation, breathing coatings, etc. to keep moisture out or to expell moisture.

4. Durability

4.1 Resistance to wear

    4.1.1 Abrasion resistance   ASTM C501

    4.1.2 Resistance to scratching   Pencil hardness test

4.2 Weathering

    4.2.1 Weather resistance   ASTM C217

    4.2.2 Freeze-thaw   ASTM C666

    4.2.3 Acid resistance   ASTM D543

    4.2.4 Appearance after weathermeter test   ASTM G–23

4.3 Adhesion of coatings

    4.3.1 Delamination   ASTM C481

Note: Since resistance to wear and weathering appear to be low, applied coatings and coverings are essential. Recommended coatings and coverings must be chosen and selected to safeguard the basic material from the effects of wear and weather.

5. Practicability

5.1 Transport

    5.1.1 Limitations with respect to size, weight, handling   Analysis/physical simulation

5.2 Storage on site

CHART 11. Evaluation of Siporex as an Exterior Wall (Continued)

Requirement	Criterion	Test Method	Result
	5.2.1 Protective against elements		Must be protected from water
	5.3 Handling during installation		
	5.3.1 Abrasion		Patching methods essential to overcome these problems
	5.3.2 Breakage		
	5.3.3 Scaring		
	5.4 Field tolerances		
	5.4.1 Corrective measures		Material readily cut in field.
	5.5 Dimensional stability		
	5.5.1 Warpage due to: Heat Wetting	Analysis/physical situation	
	5.6 Connections		
	5.6.1 Inserts		
6. Maintenance	6.1 Compatibility of Coatings		
	6.1.1 Interaction		
	6.1.2 Delamination		

Note: Inserts must be corrosion resistant. Connections must develop pull-out resistance anticipated.

6.2 Graffiti
Resistance
    6.2.1 Ability to resist and
            clean

6.3 Indentation and
Puncture
    6.3.1 Patching Materials

Note: Recommended coatings must be investigated to ascertain compatibility and resistance to graffiti attack. Patching methods must be simple and effective.

7. Compatability

7.1 Jointing
Materials
    7.1.1 Adherance of   Fed. Spec. TT-S-227
            sealants
    7.1.2 Staining of sealants

7.2 Coatings
    7.2.1 Ability to receive   ASTM C481
            and retain coatings

7.3 Galvanic
Interaction
or Corrosion
Resistance of
inserts and
attachments

CHART 11. Evaluation of Siporex as an Exterior Wall (Continued)

Requirement	Criterion	Test Method	Result
	7.3.1 Steel	Physical simulation	
	7.3.2 Aluminum	tests	
	7.3.3 Wood		
	7.3.4 Metallic conduit		

Note: Applied coatings, sealants, inserts and adjacent materials must be investigated for compatibility.

Evaluation of Siporex as a Floor-Ceiling-Roof and Partition

Note: See Requirements for Siporex as an Exterior Wall Material. Add the following requirements.

Requirement	Criterion	Test Method	Results
1. Acoustic properties	1.1 Impact Sound	Topping Machine ISO R140	
2. Structural	2.1 Impact Resistance	ASTM E72	
	2.2 Occupancy Loads		
	2.3 Deflection		
	2.4 Concentrated Loads		
3. Compatibility	3.1 Adhesive Floor Coverings		
	3.2 Chemical Resistance		
4. Habitability	4.1 Floor Coverings Moisture Protection	Fed Spec. TT-C-00555	

CHART 12.   Test Methods Cited in Chart 11

ASTM Test Methods

C140   Sampling & Testing Concrete Masonry Units

C177   Thermal Conductivity of Materials by Means of the Guarded Hot
Plate

C217   Weather Resistance of Natural Slate

C355   Water Vapor Transmission Rate of Thick Materials

C423   Sound Absorption of Acoustical Materials in Reverberation Rooms

C426   Drying Shrinkage of Concrete Block

C481   Laboratory Aging of Sandwich Construction

C501   Resistance to Wear of Unglazed Ceramic Tile by Taber Abraser

C666   Freeze-Thaw Test

C683   Compressive & Flexural Strength of Concrete

D543   Resistance of Plastic to Chemical Reagents

E72   Strength Tests of Panels for Building Construction

E84   Surface Burning Characteristics of Building Materials

E90   Laboratory Measurement of Airborne Sound Transmission Loss

E119   Fire Tests of Building Construction and Materials

E228   Linear Thermal Expansion of Rigid Solids

E514   Water Permeability of Masonry

G23   Carbon-Arc Weathermeter Test for Non-Metallic Materials

---

Federal Standard

Animal Inhalation Test—Federal Hazardous Substances Act

Judgment, Simulation and Experience

At the beginning of this chapter it was noted that for some performance characteristics, notably "practicability," the assessment is usually based on judgement, simulation, and/or experience.

The same observation and assessment might be appropriate to certain materials or products. A case in point is waterproofing. To fathom the problems associated with waterproofing and to select appropriate materials to solve various aspects of waterproofing, it is essential to utilize judgement, experience, and finally the structured analytical approach.

Since the presence of unwanted water inside a structure is a visible, annoying, and damaging element, it has spawned a host of waterproofing manufacturers, and their products are legion. Quite often manufacturers' literature in the area of waterproofing is completely devoid of factual data concerning their products and the user is faced with the difficult task of making assessments with very little information other than glowing self-serving statements.

A structure may require waterproofing at several salient and vulnerable surfaces. Chart 13 shows a typical section through a structure that has a machine room and toilet room above grade that requires waterproof floors, an exterior plaza that requires waterproofing to protect an occupied space beneath, and a basement area that is subject to a hydrostatic head of water.

CHART 13.   Cross Section of Structure

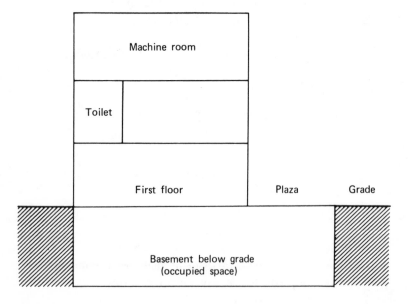

In each instance the type of waterproofing may be different and the architect must make a selection from literally dozens of materials that are available to him. To simplify the selection process, we must first classify the available waterproofing products so that a more intelligent appraisal might be achieved.

The available products can be classified as follows:

Type No.	Waterproofing System
1	Bituminous-built-up membrane Asphalt or coal tar 2, 3, 4, or 5 ply
2	Elastomeric sheet Neoprene Butyl EPDM (etheylene, propylene diamine monomer) PVC
3	Liquid applied membranes (for application between slabs and below grade walls) Polyurethane, 1 and 2 part Tar-modified polyurethane Rubberized asphalt
4	Surface applied liquid membrane (Traffic Bearing Slabs) Polyurethane Neoprene-hypalon
5	Metallic Iron fillings mixed with cement and water
6	Bentonite A granular mineral that forms a water repelling gel when in contact with moisture
7	Cementitious systems Mixtures of cements and chemical additives, which are absorbed into concrete by water causing crystallization which fills concrete pores and capillaries.
8	Integral admixtures Proprietary admixtures added to concrete mixes to render the concrete watertight

9   Proprietary systems
           Various coatings, sheets, powders, etc. that are claimed
           by their respective manufacturers to protect against pas-
           sage of water.

When we analyze the structure (Chart 13) and the nature of the waterproofing problems we can first use a modicum of judgement and experience to guide us in making a product selection.

If we start below grade with a hydrostatic head we must also ascertain whether the structure is out in the open so that the exterior of the
foundation walls are accessible for application of waterproofing or
whether the structure is in a crowded, hemmed-in urban site where
waterproofing can only be applied to the inside face of the walls and
floors of the foundation.

If the exterior walls are accessible then Types 1, 2, 3, 6, 7, and 8 are
possible candidate solutions. The next step is to determine what local
waterproofing subcontractors have been utilizing for comparable situations and with what success. Type 1, bituminous built-up membranes
are the oldest materials with some good track records and are generally
capable of being applied by most applicators. Since the other types are
of more recent vintage, they may not necessarily have local applicators
with sufficient experience to warrant their use. One must carefully assess the nature of the water problem, the geometry of the foundation,
and the local applicator's experience before making a decision to use
other than a Type 1 system.

If the foundation is hemmed in so that waterproofing can only be
applied to the inside face, the number of types available dwindles to
Types 5, 7, and 8. Here again consideration should be given to local
practices and successes. Type 5, metallic waterproofing, has been employed successfully in the New York area for deep excavations. Type 7,
cementitious systems originated in Europe, have had many successful
applications in Canada, and offer much promise. Type 7 has been
successful in water systems such as pipes, viaducts, tanks and in swim-
ming pools. Type 8, proprietory admixtures, depend, upon extremely

good concrete workmanship. The application of performance criteria in evaluating a type 8 product would be extremely difficult.

At the Plaza level in Chart 13 the objective is to waterproof the substrate immediately below the finished paved surface when there is an occupied space below grade. Several material types are possible candidate solutions. Types 1 to 3 are generally used. Type 1, bituminous built-up membranes, is the oldest with a long history; type 2, elastomeric sheet, has some 20 to 25 years of use experience; and type 3, liquid applied membranes, are of recent vintage.

Type 3 would appear to offer the best solution, since it is monolithic, is capable of being turned up, down, and around geometric shapes, is self-flashing, and is relatively economical. Its developmental history, however, parallels the introduction of elastomeric sealants some 25 years ago. Every manufacturer with a bathtub could formulate a liquid-applied membrane product and the concoctions ran the gamut from bitumen-modified polysulfides and polyurethanes to rubberized asphalt and to 100% solids polyurethanes. Criteria for a product was undefined and no standards existed by which to judge a product. Recently an ASTM standard was promulgated: ASTM C836 sets forth some important criteria such as 1) film thickness on vertical surfaces, 2) adhesion-in-peel after water immersion, 3) extensibility after heat aging, and 4) low-temperature flexibility and crack bridging. An ASTM recommended practice for application of the cold-applied liquid membranes is about to be issued. The ASTM material standard, based on performance characteristics gives the user a much better opportunity to select a liquid-applied membrane with better assurance that the product will work in a situation such as plaza waterproofing.

At the Toilet Room level in Chart 13 a membrane is required beneath ceramic tile, which is the customary finish in this particular situation. With a normal mortar setting bed, Types 1 to 3 waterproofing system and Type 9 proprietary sheet systems are all perfectly adequate. However, where there are problems in depressing slabs or where thin-set tile is desirable, there are now Type 3 liquid-applied membranes that are being formulated and are compatible with latex-modified mortars used with thin-set ceramic tile installations.

At the Machine Room level in Chart 13, the use of a waterproofing membrane was generally confined to double slabbing, i.e., placing a Type 1 membrane between slabs. Type 2 and 3 membranes will also function in a between slab configuration. However, with the advent of Type 4, surface-applied liquid membranes, the cost of double slabbing can be eliminated since a liquid neoprene and a liquid polyurethane system, which are traffic bearing can now be considered for use based on their performance characteristics.

Summary

The prospective user of materials with the aid of the rational analytical method is now in a better position to "evaluate" new products and to "select" new products for a new project from the myriad products available. This can be done on the basis of the performance concept and the procedures outlined in Charts 5 and 6. ASTM and Federal Specification test methods can be used to obtain information on physical criteria that is important and crucial in a specific instance.

Where certain aspects do not lend themselves to a performance analysis, then judgement, simulation, and experience must be employed to assess the potentials of a product.

The building material manufacturer likewise now has a tool for establishing which physical characteristics are essential in a new product for a given use and develops the required tests to obtain specific results that can be used to promote the product more successfully.

1.3

Contractor Involvement

Construction managers and contractors are often confronted with the task of making material evaluations and selections by virtue of their involvement in the construction process. Construction managers particularly must offer recommendations to bring construction projects within budget allowances. In addition, specified materials and products may often become unavailable due to strikes, shortages, or discontinuance of production by the manufacturer, forcing the contractor or construction manager to offer comparable products or substitutes.

The evaluation and selection of substitute products and materials can be achieved by contractors and construction managers on the same basis as previously outlined for the design professional.

Materials, products, and systems that have been carefully assessed as having the attributes required to perform in a given situation require one additional major ingredient to succeed, that is, its installation. Here the execution of that installation falls upon the contractor and the construction manager. Specification and manufacturers instructions must be carefully followed so that the peculiar characteristics of the selected product are achieved in the final installation and are not mitigated by improper installation. This is particularly true with respect to the installation of new products and materials although attention to details with respect to installation of older products is likewise absolutely essential.

To illustrate how contractors and construction managers should re-

45

view specifications and manufacturer's application instructions see Chart 14. (Reproduced with permission of Turner Construction Co.)

CHART 14.

ELASTOMERIC SEALANTS (CONTINUED)

TURNER CONSTRUCTION COMPANY

PERFORMANCE ESSENTIALS

FIELD CHECK LIST
FOR
ELASTOMERIC SEALANTS
07900

A. THIS CHECK LIST IS NOT INTENDED TO BE A SUBSTITUTE FOR THE ARCHITECT'S SPECIFI-CATIONS—CONSULT THEM AND PREPARE A LIST OF REQUIRED ITEMS TO BE USED IN CONJUNC-TION WITH THIS FIELD CHECK LIST.

PREPARATION

B. PRIOR TO THE START OF WORK HAVE A JOB CONFERENCE WITH ALL CONCERNED PARTIES TO ESTABLISH WORK RULES AND PROCEDURES, AND TO RECORD ANY UNSATISFACTORY CONDI-TIONS OF THE WORK. HOLD CONFERENCES THEREAFTER ON A WEEKLY BASIS OR AS REQUIRED.

SURFACES TO WHICH SEALANTS ARE TO BE APPLIED SHOULD BE DRY AND VIRGIN CLEAN. THE MOST COMMON THINGS OVERLOOKED AND WHICH WILL PREVENT OR INHIBIT ADHESION ARE:

1. CONCRETE CURING COMPOUNDS

C. MAKE SURE MATERIALS BEING USED ARE THOSE SPECIFIED OR APPROVED.

2. FORM RELEASE AGENTS

3. ASPHALTIC COMPOUNDS IN MEMBRANE SYSTEMS

D. NOTIFY SEALANT MANUFACTURER OF DATE OF START OF WORK FOR TECHNICAL GUIDANCE AT SITE AND TO PREPARE A DETAILED APPLICA-TION PROCEDURE.

4. PETROLEUM STAINS

5. LACQUERS

6. OILS, WAX, SOAP, GREASE, ETC.

E. PREPARE A MOCK-UP FOR APPROVAL.

7. PROTECTIVE COATINGS—SILICONES, ACRYLICS, STEARATES, ETC.

F. CHECK AS-BUILT JOINT DIMENSION RELATIVE TO SEALANT PERFORMANCE CAPABILITY.

8. ATMOSPHERIC DEPOSITS—OILY SOOT, CARBONS, ETC. DO NOT PERMIT CLEANING AND/OR PRIM-ING TO PROCEED TOO FAR AHEAD OF CAULKING.

G. CHECK BACK-UP MATERIAL FOR PROPER DEPTH.

9. LAITANCE, DUST, POWDER AND ALKALINE DEPOSITS.

H. ATTENTION TO PROPER JOINT PREPARATION IS ESSENTIAL FOR MAXIMUM ADHESION.

10. EXCESSIVE MOISTURE

11. IF A PRIMER IS REQUIRED FOR ADHESION, MAKE CERTAIN IT IS APPLIED.

J. THE JOINT CLEANSER MUST BE COMPATIBLE WITH THE SEALANT AND ADJOINING MATERIALS.

12. NEVER USE CLEANING SOLVENTS CONTAINING MINERAL SPIRITS AS BOND WILL THEN BE IMPOSSIBLE. USE ONLY TOLUENE, METHYL ETHYL KETONE (M.E.K.) OR XYLENE.

K. TOOLING OF THE SEALANT IS ESSENTIAL TO PROMOTE ADHESION AND THE ELIMINATION OF TRAPPED AIR WITHIN THE SEALANT.

13. LOW ATMOSPHERIC OR SURFACE TEMPERATURES. BE CERTAIN THAT MASONRY SURFACES DO NOT CONTAIN FROST OR MOISTURE CONDENSATION. BOTH PREVENT ADHESION. FOLLOW THE MANU-FACTURER'S RECOMMENDED APPLICATION TEM-PERATURE PRECAUTIONS. IF NOT READILY AVAILABLE, A RULE-OF-THUMB GUIDE IS 40°F. WITH THE TEMPERATURE RISING, NOT FALLING.

L. BLISTERS OR BUBBLING IS THE RESULT OF EXPANDING MOISTURE VAPOR. THE USUAL CAUSES ARE TRAPPED AIR IN THE SEALANT OR A POROUS BACK-UP ROD, AND THE INABILITY OF AIR TO ESCAPE OUT OF THE BACK OF THE JOINT.

14. HIGH ATMOSPHERIC OR SURFACE TEMPERATURES WILL INHIBIT OR DELAY CURING OF MOST SEALANTS; HOWEVER, DELAY APPLICATION IF POSSIBLE UNTIL THE AMBIENT TEMPERATURE IS AROUND 70°F. OTHERWISE THE JOINT WILL BE AT ITS MINIMUM DIMENSION WHICH IS DETRIMENTAL TO ULTIMATE OPTIMUM SEALANT PERFORMANCE.

M. CONDUCT STAIN TESTS FOR PRIMER OR SEALANT WHEN THEY ARE TO BE APPLIED TO A MASONRY SURFACE.

N. OCCASIONALLY IT BECOMES NECESSARY TO MASK OFF A JOINT. WHEN MASKING TAPE IS USED, IT MUST BE STRIPPED IMMEDIATELY FOLLOWING TOOLING OF THE SEALANT OR IT BECOMES BONDED TO THE SEALANT.

O. AVOID THIRD POINT SEALANT ADHESION IN ANY DYNAMIC JOINT AS FAILURE WOULD THEN BE GUARANTEED.

P. WHEN TWO-COMPONENT MATERIALS ARE USED, THE MIXING TIME BECOMES CRITICAL. BE CERTAIN THAT MIXING TIME IS ADHERED TO AND THAT PROPER MIXING PADDLES ARE USED.

READ THE CONSTRUCTION BULLETIN AND DIGESTS ON SEALANTS

Chart 14 for elastomeric sealants is one of a series of field checklists that have been developed by Turner Construction Company as an aid to their field personnel in the installation of materials. The field checklist is a result of experience with the installation of a material, manufactuer's input, and highlights that have been gleaned from various project specifications. It contains information that oftentimes is not included in a specification. While a specification may call for clean joint surfaces, the Turner field checklist cites 14 separate joint conditions that may affect the proper adhesion of an elastomeric sealant. The point to remember is that although the design professional may have correctly evaluated and selected a product, its improper installation would vitiate all the benefits that would have been derived from the characteristics of the product.

Furthermore, the checklist reminds the field personnel to review the architect's specification for additional requirements and to perform such additional tasks to assure maximum performance from a product. Again it is imperative that field personnel involved in supervision establish a routine for highlighting critical aspects of installation to assure a trouble-free finished product.

The last reference on Chart 14 to read construction bulletins and digests refers to a Turner in-house manual that has been developed for most building products and systems and cites reference sources, articles, papers, and standards that bear on the specific product.

While this book deals with a rational appproach to construction materials evaluation and selection it is appropriate that a similar organized matrix be developed for classifying and cataloging the do's and dont's or pitfalls of materials installation so that the contractor and construction manager be in a better position to deal with their successful installation.

PART TWO

Developing the Systematic Approach to Construction Material Evaluation and Selection

PHILIP M. BENNETT

2.1   **The Need, 53**
    Historic Account of Material Use, 53
    Number of Materials Used in Different Time Periods, 53

    Chart 15   Chronological Development and Use of Natural and Man-Made Construction Materials—A Technological Change to Greater Dependency on Human Performance, 57

    Number of People Involved in Design and Construction Stages, 57
    Changes in Design Due to Life Style, 59
    Public Demand and Liabilities Placed on Designers, Manufacturers, and Contractors, 61

2.2   **The Systematic Approach, 63**
The Mental Process of Decision-Making, 63
Personal Responsibilities and Organization of Information, 64
The Decision-Making Program, 65
Information Collection and Organization, 68
Feedback and Monitoring Programs, 70
Building Research Programs, 71

Chart 16   Essential Steps of an Effective Field Feedback
Program, 71
Chart 17   Field Feedback and Test Results Provide Crucial
Information for Product and Material Evaluation
Processes, 72

Techniques For Developing a Systematic Approach, 73

2.3   **System Development, 75**
Objectives and Goals of Program, 75
Human Capability to Develop an Organized Approach, 76
System Development Based on Areas of Impact, 78
Identification of Performance Criteria, 81

Chart 18   Stages Where Possible Failures Occur in the Development
and Use of Products and Materials, 83

Weighting Performance Criteria, 84

Chart 19   Critical Steps in the Product and Material Evaluation and
Selection Process, 86

Use of a Matrix for Information Relationships, 86

Chart 20   Developing a Building Material Evaluation Matrix, 87
Chart 21   Building Material Evaluation Matrix and Rating Sheet, 88
Chart 22   Rating Key for Building Material Evaluation Matrix and
Rating Sheet, 91
Chart 23   Using the Building Material Evaluation Matrix, 91
Chart 24   Building Material Evaluation, 93

Building Material Evaluation Matrix Capabilities, 94
A Manual or Computerized Evaluation Matrix, 94
Benefits of a Computer Program for Material/Product Evaluation and
Selection, 95

Chart 25   Building Material Evaluation Matrix and Rating
            Sheet, 96

2.4   **Responsibilities of the Design Professional, 98**
Client Expectations, 98
Professional Responsibilities, 99
Team Work Requirements, 100
Future Role of Design Professionals, 102
Legal Responsibilities, 103

2.5   **Use of a Systematic Approach, 107**
Application of a Systematic Approach by the Building Design
Team, 107
Exploring the Evaluation and Selection Options, 108

Chart 26   Product Attributes, 109

Client Input and Responsibility, 116
Management and Organization of Information, 118
Legal Implications of Using a Systematic Approach, 119
A Systematic Approach to Achieve Building Material
Performance, 127

Glossary, 131
References, 133

2.1

The Need

Historic Account of Material Use

For many centuries, people's decisions about their environment and natural resources directly affected their survival. Earlier cultures were limited by available materials and instruments by which necessary shelters could be constructed. Yet some of the finest artisanship and perfection in the use of materials was prevalent when laborers had only stone and wood to construct living and working environments.

Throughout history stone was always a major building material. Marble, travertine, and other natural stones were used in ancient Egyptian and Greek temples. There was a great span of time from when the Romans developed brick and concrete before other new building materials were discovered. During this wide interval, skills in working with each material were perfected. The best available construction skills and building technology were employed and perfected to provide places of religious and protective architecture.

Number of Materials Used in Different Time Periods

The development of steel and other composition building materials introduced human performance as a new variable in material production. Steel as a material brought about a tremendous change in architecture. As natural resources were combined to provide greater strength in construction, products and materials became dependent upon human capabilities.

Today's designers must make material selections from an ever-increasing variety of new building products and materials. This phenomenal explosion of products is beyond efficient assessment by using present evaluation techniques. Modern building materials must be systematically analyzed by design professionals to arrive at the most skillful use and application of modern materials in construction. In the past 20 years alone there has been a radical increase in building design and construction problems due to some of the following conditions:

- A tremendous change in technology.
- A rapid increase in the introduction of new building materials and products.
- A major increase in new construction information.
- A change in legal responsibilities.
- A greater complexity in facility requirements.

Problems that have evolved have changed the design process and increased building construction costs. The construction environment of the last 20 years has created a new frontier of professional responsibilities. Changes in technology have resulted in more personal responsibility for the design professional. The design professional must consider working with other construction professionals to develop a building team. This team, working together, using all the basic knowledge and available information, can make effective decisions in the design and construction process.

The development of many synthetic products has increased the complexity of the building industry during the last several decades. Products that result from combinations of natural resources, human performance, and technological capabilities, have increased the potential for problems to occur. These problems have increased as quickly as the number of products. Testing and research for evaluation has not been able to keep pace with the number of newly developed products. This enables products to be used or marketed before the design professional can be assured that the products do indeed fulfill the desired requirements.

Human performance is a major variable in a new product and can cause the performance to vary from established standards or the client's expectations. The materials used, mixing, curing, temperature changes, and the environment in which the product was produced, are all variables that can affect the way a product will perform. Research studies have identified as many as 60 variables in the development and placement of concrete. In some cases these variables are so great that it is difficult to control human actions during the production period. Other variables occur when the product is subjected to the elements in its environment. Some variables in synthetic products are:

- Human performance in product design.
- Natural resources selected to develop the product.
- Methods used to produce the product.
- Available labor for producing the product.
- Experience of the craftsmen involved in producing the product.
- Production time or limitations.
- Quality control over the production process.
- Product application and installation.
- Control over the use of the product.

The design professional must begin to utilize all of the available information to develop methods of quality control in the design, manufacturing, and construction of the building. A performance comparison between the synthetic products and natural materials will show that the frequency of problems has been mainly due to the number of human variables involved in the production and assembly or installation process. Natural materials have weathered environmental forces with few performance variables. The performance of recently manufactured synthetic products has been difficult to predict because of our lack of field experience, especially since little is known on how the product will react chemically to changes in the natural environment. There is not sufficient time to test products for long periods because of rapid changes in technology and client demands, thus requiring the construction industry to react more quickly than the builder of many centuries ago.

Contemporary architects and engineers use hundreds of materials and products. If all of the human variables and number of products used are taken into account, it can be seen that the designer has little control over the final performance of a building. Chart 15 plots the number of materials used during the Egyptian period, down through centuries of building construction. By the nineteenth century, there had been a great increase in the number of products and building materials. An Egyptian temple was basically made of one material. The typical office building in a modern business district is made of at least five natural materials and virtually hundreds of synthetic products. This complexity of modern architecture requires the work of many different disciplines. If there is to be some form of quality control over the final performance, communication with consultants and specialists who have gained firsthand experience in working with products and materials is needed. One person alone cannot acquire the amount of information needed to make effective and successful judgements about all materials and building products available in today's world.

CHART 15. Chronological Development and use of Natural and Manmade Construction Materials—A Technological Change to Greater
Dependency on Human Performance

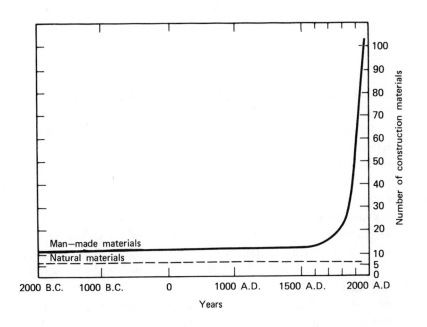

Number of People Involved in Design and Construction Stages

The number of people involved in the design and construction of recent
buildings is many times greater than during past construction. During
various stages of building construction there are hundreds of people
interacting. The result of their work is dependent upon the total communication, coordination, and cooperation on the part of each team
member. If one construction segment does not fulfill its task competently, the performance of a building can be altered. Under the Master
Builder concept, one person designed the building and was the key
element to its construction. The Master Builder was in charge of design

and construction; many other artisans were involved in the final construction, under the Master Builder's direction. Today, segments of the construction team must work under many different time and economic constraints during stages of design and construction. This work arrangement complicates the work, and requires other individuals to develop Master Builder skills. Architects and engineers are now designing buildings when technological change is greater than in any other time in history. New building materials and products must perform according to written specifications or the designer will be called to account for misjudgement in selection. The energy crisis and higher material costs compel users to accept products of lesser quality and reduced performance capabilities. This makes the selection process even more critical. Much greater emphasis will be placed on performance aspects of all materials used by the construction industry in the future.

Changing consumer attitudes and awareness have helped to create an era of legal problems in design and construction. The designer and specifier are becoming more accountable for building performance. Each material researcher and selector must have greater knowledge and experience in building material performance to cope with increased responsibilities. Greater responsibilities are being placed on all members of the design, manufacturing, and construction team. It is incumbent upon every member of the team to perform a given task to the best of his or her ability.

Many problems can occur in the design stages. There can be problems of misunderstandings between client and architect, between designer and job captains and draftsmen. There can also be misunderstandings between the design and specification team. It is the responsibility of those involved in the design and selection process to understand the problems that might result by using a particular material or product. Yet responsibility must be shared by the manufacturing team, who are responsible for developing new construction products. The manufacturing process has changed drastically over the last few years. There are increasing numbers of people working on the development of new products which in turn requires many more skilled workers in product manufacturing. Mass production and assemblyline types of manufacturing centers have arisen due to increased user needs. In these centers, there are thousands of people performing daily tasks that affect the final product and its performance in a particular building. There are many variables and people involved in the performance areas, and responsibilities must be shared by the total building team.

The technological changes that have taken place over the last few decades makes it beyond human comprehension to understand all of the problems that might evolve through the use of one product. There must be constant testing and monitoring by all disciplines involved in the design, manufacturing, and construction process. These activities have become a science in itself, known as "building technology." To keep updated requires constant involvement in self-education and continuing education, researching, field monitoring, and in building evaluation. Every stage and phase of work must be documented so that new findings and problem areas can be dealt with as quickly as possible. Only through effective feedback systems can correction methods that will not be time-lagging be incorporated into job performance. Quality-control systems need to be developed that save time and money for designers and clients.

Changes in Design Due to Life Style

Due to technology, daily living patterns have changed. The lead-time required to develop new products and move them from one area of the country to another has been drastically reduced. An idea can be sketched on paper one day, within the week it is possible to have a mock-up of the product, and in a month or two it can be on the production line. Technology has had a tremendous impact upon the actual performance of any one individual. Because of rapid changes and automation in many areas of job performance, certain real skills have been lost.

New building systems and construction techniques to solve present space needs have to be developed. Engineering and design skills need to be directed toward making construction methods more efficient and economical. Complexity in facility requirements also makes it imperative that design professionals develop better methods of identifying user needs so that more effective design solutions can emerge. Every member of the building design, construction, and manufacturing team should work together to develop new products to satisfy changing user needs. New material shortages, energy sources, and high costs of production requires the cooperation and new technique development from the construction industry. Technological problems will have a tremendous impact upon the construction and manufacturing industry, forcing designers to acquire new ways of working together for analyzing problems and approach solutions systematically to develop a manmade environment. Some of the changing needs and ways interior space is being used will reduce the amount needed to perform certain tasks. For example, residences used for part-time offices incorporate the work environment into that of the living environment. In the future, there may be changes that will bring workers back into the residential community with their occupational skills and possibly create products without traveling far from their home. Increased costs for physical space will reduce the availability of synthetic environments for human performance. This will compel the design professional to be more selective in identifying user needs in programming space for future use.

Design responsibilities will increase as clients expect performances that provide environments that fulfill the many contemporary complex needs of living. As the needs and complexity increase, so will responsibilities. Design professionals must look for new ways of organizing information and obtaining necessary feedback for making good judgements. Many lifestyle changes affect design through impacts in:

- Transportation
- Communication
- Building Technology
- Time constraints

- Economic limitations
- Material availability
- Energy availability
- Skills

- Laws and Codes
- Labor practices
- Construction practices
- Environmental standards

The complexity of these changes requires that they be dealt with systematically in the decision-making process. Major constraints such as material availability and costs require that design professionals work cooperatively with clients and consultants to clarify needs, priorities, and design options. Critical information must be identified and evaluated to provide the client with the best performance for money and effort expended.

Public Demands and Liabilities Placed on Designers, Manufacturers, and Contractors

Job requirements and labor costs have become so immense that clients no longer tolerate poor capabilities from synthetic materials or products. The manufacturer or seller must now prove that a product will perform as specified and be responsible for its shortcomings. Changes in the public demand, law, and relationship between the seller and buyer, force the designer to reassess his position in the field of merchandising. The design professionals' position from the clients' viewpoint has become that of the seller, manufacturer, the person in charge of developing the whole product (facility) and therefore totally responsible for its final performance. As a building developer, the design professional must respond when called upon to evaluate why a product does not perform the way the client expects. Trends occurring in legislation, i.e., new safety and environmental laws, are having a tremendous impact upon the producer, the seller, and the builder in general. The future will place greater responsibility upon the design professional and team to perform in a competent manner. It will require greater clarification of user requirements, performance capabilities, and limitations, and performance agreed upon and contracted for. Negligent professionals will encounter tremendous problems, legal suits, and even work stoppage because shoddy performance will not be tolerated.

New certification and accreditation programs are being developed by many states and communities. They are specifying performance levels and the requirements for design professionals and others providing a public service. Legal changes will alter ways design professionals work with other members of the construction industry team. The designer, manufacturer, and construction representative must work together to clarify problem areas before they influence the performance of a final product. Through total cooperation, and a better understanding of user needs, products can be manufactured and facilities built that achieve greater client satisfaction. Errors and liabilities will be reduced by achieving a higher level of performance on the part of the design and construction team. Both design and construction team members must make every effort to systematically gather feedback from field problems, product and facility evaluation information, and related tests and research in order to prevent improper application and installation of products and materials. The design professional and team members must take the precautions to systematically gather feedback from recent field problems and research to carry out a competent design performance. A systems approach to problem solving in design and selection will encourage a higher level of performance for each discipline in the construction industry.

2.2

The Systematic Approach

The Mental Process of Decision-Making

Design professionals in a technological world are faced with very complex and interrelated problems that require a great deal of information to make a good decision. How does one make a decision or form a judgement about a problem? If all of the information and knowledge that is presently available when making up a mental decision is taken into account, the decision process is conducted systematically. The criteria used to make a decision is based upon a feedback system. The mind recalls information of prior decisions and then reorganizes the information to make a new decision. This mental process can be improved if good information is gathered and organized to have new input to the human mind. Electronics, mechanical equipment, computers, or technological means are not required to perform systematically. All that is needed is good information, acquired through reading, through researching, through testing, or by direct observation. Once this information has been documented and catalogued, the mental process can take over in making a good judgement.

Human performance can be systematic. Good judgement is usually arrived at systematically and if this process is used it may be said that the design professional is operating competently. If they do not utilize prior knowledge and existing information, there are negligent operations. It is easy to operate and make decisions subjectively because that is what comes naturally. Good judgement and prior information gathering is required to perform effectively and make good, objective decisions. Decisions made systematically based on sound information will usually stand up in a court of law. In all cases, a design professional is only expected to perform in a competent manner using the latest information at hand. That information is usually based on prior experience and conventional systems that have been known to perform effectively over a period of time. If the design professional operates systematically, clients will acquire greater service, and have respect for the performance.

Personal Responsibilities and Organization of Information

Making decisions for clients requires a great deal of preparation of information and experience about problems. In many cases it requires a great deal of time and effort for the design professional. Design professionals should take personal responsibility for making sure the proper investigations into the past have been made. There is so much information available on many subjects, that it may take hours, days, even months to identify, catalogue, and systematically select those areas of information that are relevant for a particular problem. It requires a skillful researcher to find the right information and the most valuable information. In many cases, in the larger firm, it is best to hire a competent person in the field of research as an assistant. Even small firms starting a library or information center should be able to afford a part-time or multidisciplined person to take charge of information handling and research. In the future, a design professional will be forced to conduct research and investigation-type activities to make successful decisions about client problems.

Information availability and documentation is growing at a rate beyond comprehension. In the future, design professionals will be dependent on construction information systems, computer selection, and retrieval systems to select information that has been catalogued under certain subject areas. These types of systems enable the designer to make better decisions because a greater volume of information has been documented on a given problem. Once the information is available, it must be organized in a logical manner. Information by itself does not give an answer. Collected information must be sorted and selected for relevancy. The design professional must learn when to seek new information and where to go to find the most valuable information that is available on a particular subject. This is a serious personal responsibility. Areas where information might be attained systematically are as follows:

- Construction information systems.
- Library centers.
- Building performance evaluation.
- Building research centers.
- Testing laboratories.
- University research centers.

Such facilities and organizations can give the design professional additional support for making the proper decisions.

The Decision-Making Program

The design professional's responsibility toward decision-making is dependent upon a systematic approach. To develop a personal approach requires a great deal of research and investigation as to how the designer is operating as an individual in the design profession. The type of design service that is provided, the clientele, and type of decisions must all be taken into account. Once positions and responsibilities have been identified and analyzed, an effective program for systematically making good design decisions can then be developed. Two questions design professionals should ask of themselves are: "Am I systematically identifying an approach that will enable me or my firm to do a better job in material selection and evaluation? Am I taking into account all the areas of concern that influence the selection process?" Other factors that must be taken into account are as follows:

- Is material performance information being systematically recorded?
- Is there a monitoring system and field feedback service?
- Is it possible to identify and develop a field feedback system that will bring in valuable construction performance information?
- Are other construction projects observed and evaluated?
- Are literature and building evaluation reports that are published followed?
- Does the company receive mailing lists for publications that continue to prepare information about building products and building technology?
- Is it known how the material used in previous jobs is performing at the present time?
- Is information from building maintenance departments being collected?

Thinking about and answering such questions will facilitate decision making. Such questions can serve as a reminder to locate the critical areas for gaining the type of information to make effective decisions about client problems. The design professional and other members of the design team can carry out many activities and tasks to become more organized and systematic in the decision-making process:

- Monitor job progress and building performance.
- Develop an effective field feedback system using key personnel to contribute valuable field findings.
- Obtain papers and research reports from various building research centers across the nation.
- Have material tested for various projects being worked on.

- Identify performance requirements for specific applications of various types of materials.

- Ask manufacturers to present all of the pertinent information available on the particular product that is under consideration.

- Have manufacturers' representatives on the job when the particular product or material is applied or installed.

- Have field men document all activities that occurred on the job during the time of product installation.

- Develop an effective library and cataloging system on all information collected on building materials and research findings.

- Develop an index that identifies all research centers and testing programs so quick identification and investigation can be carried out with little loss of time.

- Obtain feedback from building maintenace departments that keep records on material and product performance.

These are some of the activities that the design professional can carry out to make competent design decisions for his client. It is not expected that everyone can carry out all of these activities efficiently and effectively at all times. Yet an effort to accomplish a number of these activities will improve the design professional's ability to perform effectively. Client respect will be gained for making an effort to institute these criteria to provide a better service. Each step in the decision-making process should be documented so other members of the organization can follow them systematically. If all team members are working under the same system and with the same goals in mind, it will be much easier for everyone to communicate effectively when faced with making material selection or building design decisions. Once procedures have been documented, they will be able to be tested and modified, resulting in an improvement in decision-making performance. Testing the system for making effective decisions is crucial in making long-range projections for new building construction.

The future of the design profession will only become more complex in the years ahead. The earlier the information-collection and decision-making process is systematized, the better. When time is at a minimum, prior planning and organization can alleviate job pressure. Valuable resources of past experience will be wasted if documentation is absent. Past experience is not easy to retrieve once passed by. There is no easier and less expensive way of building in-house education than to build experience and incorporate into the system a means for carrying out continuing education. No substitute exists for past information when it comes to making effective design decisions. History has shown that excellent design decisions can be made from earlier experiences.

Information Collection and Organization

Vast volumes of information are being produced every day. There is so much that the design professional must be very selective in the information identification process. Information gathering in itself will not give all the answers. It is important to develop an information collection system that is relevant to the type of problems that the design professional faces. Several national-level construction information systems have been developed and are available for use by the design professional.

- COMSPEC Services, Washington, D.C.
- IDAC Project Information Clearinghouse, New York, New York.
- Information Handling Service, Englewood, Colorado.
- McGraw-Hill Information Systems Company, New York, New York.
- National Technical Information Service, Washington, D.C.
- Production Systems for Architects and Engineers, Inc., Washington, D.C.
- Showcase Corporation, Detroit, Michigan.
- The Construction Specifications Institute's Programs Spec-Data I and II, Washington, D.C.

- U.S. Army Construction Engineering Research Laboratory, Champaign, Illinois.

As in-house programs are developed, it will be necessary to take advantage of operational systems. Companies should build upon the information readily available and consistent with their library and retrieval system, while being compatible with systems in use in the construction industry. Some design firms employ research specialists, material evaluators, and other individuals with building material research capabilities. In the future, design professionals will be encouraged to use specialists and construction information systems to seek out accurate design and research data for making good building material selection decisions. Once an effective in-house system is operational, it will be easier for every member of the design team to become involved in the design-selection process. A good library system will contain documentation of past material performance. This will enable the designer to build up a vast body of knowledge relevant to a particular material or product and how that the information is trustworthy. The designer who is working with a good information system will become more knowledgeable in using new materials and making good decisions. The design professional may then have foresight in regard to possible difficulties when planning new facilities. The use of material and product performance records with documented problems will facilitate improved design decisions and judgements. A systematic organization of information is vital to successful operation of design firms who must make major decisions about the use of new building materials and products. The future encourages new product development and the use of new systems. It will be imperative to document and develop effective retrieval systems for valuable information linked to changes in building technology. If an information documentation system is developed simultaneously with technological change, it will be easier for the construction industry to locate past problems. It will also facilitate predicting potential problem areas, and areas where manufacturing organizations must improve products.

Feedback and Monitoring Programs

One excellent means of obtaining material performance information is via effective field feedback programs. Many firms already have successful programs in operation that save them time and allow them to provide a better service for clients. They are able to take advantage of past and daily experiences. Firms that have specialists in the field who are able to recognize problems quickly and provide documentation are in a better position to react to the designer's needs in the office. Response to a field problem, followed by a quick feedback to the designer, is most critical in a firm that is doing many different projects over a relatively short time span. Firms with feedback programs can build valuable collections of building material information for future reference.

Performance records differ from research and test findings because they do not always relate material to the natural environment to which it is finally subjected. In an actual field condition, an accurate account of how the product performs in a natural environment over time can be obtained. Office data banks that contain descriptions of field problems can be valuable resources of information to the designer, job captain, and draftsmen. This information will also be valuable to specification writers who must made some of the final decisions about products and material application before drawing up final contract documents. If the in-house data banks contain no information, a researcher can then pursue field testing, information data centers, or checking with consultants and specialists.

The development of standard procedures for recording field information on product performance is essential to data bank effectiveness and the design professionals' organization of a systematic approach to decision making. Step-by-step procedures are important so fieldmen, designers, draftsmen, specification writers, and all individuals gathering information are using standardized methods and procedures for gathering information. Establishing a logical and systematic approach to gathering pertinent information and organizing it in a manner that will aid the information user in making effective design decisions. Some of the essential steps are listed in Chart 16.

CHART 16.   Essential Steps of an Effective Field Feedback Program

1   Develop an acceptable information documentation format
2   Produce guidelines for recording information
3   Establish a cataloging system to record, store, and retrieve gathered information
4   Specify the key personnel who will be responsible for maintaining an active feedback program
5   Systematize a procedure for disseminating field feedback information to the appropriate personnel.

Building Research Programs

Building material research programs are increasing in private offices across the United States and abroad (see the Appendix). These programs are beginning to supply information about building material performance in actual environmental situations. A number of departments of the federal government are also creating research centers and laboratories to test building materials and new products. This information can have a tremendous impact on future products, and the type of materials used in building systems. Many of the research findings will have implications for the design professional in charge of building materials selections. Some of the new building systems in different areas of the nation and in foreign countries have been proven to be ineffective in fulfilling intended performance levels. By utilizing current research reports, designers can prevent making errors in product selection that may cause serious problems for the client.

Many past errors and building failures have occurred because the designer/selector did not take recorded field experience into account that was stored in someone else's files. Through the development of successful research and documentation programs, advantage of historic information can be taken to prevent serious future building con-

struction problems, see Chart 17. Privately established research organizations can give the design professional the potential to work with
specialists or consultants during early stages in the design-decision
making process. Building models can be developed, tested, and valuable performance information recorded on a material's response to the
proposed environment. Some testing agencies have been conducting
successful product and material tests over the past several years, acquiring excellent volumes of valuable construction information. When
dealing with large building projects, it is expecially important to utilize
research specialists at very early stages in the building material selection process. Their valuable background of experience can enable designers to make successful design decisions at lower costs. Systematically using research experience in the decision-making process
will also give clients added satisfaction and confidence in the designer's
professional ability.

**CHART 17.   Field Feedback and Test Results Provide Crucial
Information for Product and Material Evaluation Processes**

Results from testing are short-term exposure indicators.

- Performance
- Compatibility
- Environmental Impacts
- Strengths and Weaknesses
- Fire Safety
- Resistance

Results from field feedback are both short- and long-term exposure indicators

- Installation Problems
- Functional Performance
- Compatibility
- Environmental Impacts
- Material Failures
- Design Acceptibility
- Client and User Satisfaction

Techniques for Developing a Systematic Approach

Each design professional has a responsibility to create a systematic approach for solving design problems. In developing an approach to decision making, the techniques used in system ayalysis programs and decision-making models should be studied. Some of these techniques and guidelines can be combined with those gained by observing others performing in similar situations. Each person who carries great responsibilities in decision making has usually acquired successful techniques and approaches. If these traits are emulated, it may be possible to improve decision making and problem solving. Guidelines for developing a systematic decision making process are as follows:

- Do a task analysis of the steps and procedures used to make design and material selection decisions.
- Identify steps that can be reorganized and systematized to make a logical process from past experiences.
- Identify steps where documented findings, field feedback and research information can be put in to the decision-making process.
- Specify areas where the decision-making process can be based on objective findings rather than subjective thinking.
- Locate steps in the decision-making process that can be easily tested and the results compared to projected performance criteria.
- Analyze decision-making models to determine whether their concepts can be applied to design problems. Some examples are operation research, mathematical models, systems analysis, factor analysis, and matrix analysis.
- Define steps in the decision-making process that can take advantage of systems feedback during the decision-making process.
- Utilize equipment to program the information used in the decision-making process.
- Identify points in the decision-making process where specialists or consultants can interact.

These guidelines can enable the design professional to look at personal responsibilities in the decision-making process and analyze each step necessary to produce good results. Designers can improve the process by examining the mental steps of information retrieval, organization, selection, and decision making. Self-analysis is a personal responsibility of every individual in a decision-making role.

2.3

System Development

Objectives and Goals of Program

Technological change and legal responsibilities in building construction are requiring design professionals to develop a systems approach to the selection of building materials. The purpose, objectives, steps, and procedures used in the process must be defined before a systematic approach can be developed. If goals are clearly identified, design professionals will be able to develop steps in a process for selecting building materials to satisfy user requirements. The first requirement is to look at objectives and procedures necessary for a successful evaluation and selection process. The major objectives that must be identified and fulfilled are as follows:

1. User requirements.
2. Performance issues associated with building materials, products, and systems.
3. Performance criteria for evaluating and selecting building materials.
4. Ranked performance requirements for more effective selection.
5. A systematic method for selecting building materials, products, and systems.
6. Major sources of information on performance testing, research, and evaluation techniques.

7. Effective selection techniques that will accomplish the goals associated with a particular field of building material selection.
8. Methods of improving the total performance of all building components through the use of more effective selection techniques.

When specific objectives are defined, professionals will then be alerted to necessary stages in building material evaluation and selection processes. These stages should be incorporated into a systematic approach that contains latest research findings, knowledge, and experience gained from prior experience with building materials and products. A comprehensive and systematic approach for every member of the design profession responsible for selecting building materials ought to be a high-priority goal.

New technology in communication and research can assist the design professionals who are attempting to locate information for structuring a systematic approach. Contemporary literature identifies several systems approaches in related fields that have been constructed to assist design professionals to make product or material evaluations. Some have been developed by military and building research centers around the world. Building research stations in foreign countries such as Great Britain and The Netherlands have organized building material evaluation committees to define performance criteria and standards for assorted types of building materials and products. These performance considerations can provide designers with a basis for developing a systems approach to the decision-making process. The systems approach enables the designer and material selector to go categorically through a decision-making process, arriving at a final selection that reflects a comprehensive professional approach.

Human Capability to Develop an Organized Approach

Current and accurate information plays a major role in good decision making. Design professionals now have the capability and the communication technology to develop organized approaches to take advantage of the available research, experience, and new knowledge in building sciences. Recent changes in technology have produced the capability for design professionals to utilize instruments of communication and programming. The television, telephone, and computer are all means for storing, retrieving, and collecting information. Once a systematic approach is developed, communication techniques and information systems can be utilized by design professionals to solve client problems within time and budget constraints. Organizations and individuals who operate in a systematic manner, using all available information, are able to develop successful solutions that fulfill clients' needs. The resulting building environments stimulate and support the activities of clients and employees.

Advantage of existing systems of operation used by large organizations to coordinate the work performance of many different individuals to accomplish a complex task can be utilized as a model to construct a decision-making system. Organizations with complex tasks and activities require systems and systematic approaches in their operation so employees can fulfill goals with the least effort, cost, and time. Programs such as operation research and other systematic approaches can provide new concepts for instituting effective decision-making techniques and design judgements. Organizations that have spent time to research and develop systematic approaches have shown a very marked change to employee performance and task fulfillment.

The military has developed many types of system approaches to perform complex activities that are part of their research programs. Many have been documented in published manuals available for public use. By studying the military's research programs, the design professional can see various techniques that are applicable to complex problems of building material evaluation and selection. The most important system considerations are the steps that must be followed to arrive at final decisions utilizing all the available information provided through research, field feedback, and experience. By taking an organized and systematic approach, many departments, organizations, and the armed services have solved complex problems through effective decision-making processes. These organizations have benefited greatly by taking the time to specify all of the necessary steps to fulfill a goal. The design professional's task can be accomplished with much less effort, cost, and time if available information is organized and a decision-making process to systematically make design decisions and materials selections is used.

System Development Based on Areas of Impact

Problem analysis is an important first step in identifying issues that affect decision stages of a material selection process. The final performance of a material or product should be the main concern of the design professional. Performance is the product's ability to respond to user needs and environmental impacts. It is the manner of its fulfillment of all the important requirements set forth by the client. Performance can be measured once criteria for evaluating variables in the selected building material are defined.

The performance of a material is its inherent capability to meet functional requirements set forth by the user. By listing performance variables, selected areas can be tested to determine which may have the greatest impact on the final performance. To weigh performance variables, all important areas of performance that impact on design solutions needs to be considered. These performance areas result from established user needs. User needs are requirements in building design that should provide an environment that supports, shelters, and stimulates the users of a facility. User needs can be sorted into various categories:

1. *The Physiological Needs:* These are the basic physical requirements that are generated by survival and daily living.
2. *The Social Needs:* These are the human requirements produced by political, economical, and cultural standards of society.
3. *The Psychological Needs:* These are the perceived human requirements generated by social pressures, reaction to the environment, and mental attitudes or states of minds.

These basic user needs can be further broken down according to Maslow's theory on human needs that must be satisfied by a living and working environment. The needs, values, and goals of the user produce the performance requirements for building materials and products. The designer must recognize cultural and technological changes that will create a change in needs during the life span of the building. The most difficult factor to manage when structuring design and performance criteria for evaluating future performance of the building materials is its degree of change. The level of product performance is difficult to define and solve. Some design parameters and conditions can be projected, but immediate user needs should not be forgotten in the process. These needs can best be satisfied when they are stated as daily human performance requirements.

User needs and design parameters must be identified systematically in conjunction with constraints established by work standards. Activity or task demands are important determinants in regard to a successful design solution. The design professional who takes into account physical, social, and psychological constraints, will be demonstrating a professional approach to solving problems of the clients. The design professional can best proceed to select building materials that will satisfy performance requirements once client goals and needs are defined.

Environmental factors are the physical conditions of the surrounding environment, (exterior or interior) that affect the final performance of a given material or product through time. The impact of these factors provides major support for developing a process for selecting building materials and products. Air, water, fire, loads, wind forces, and temperature change are some variables that must be taken into account when performance requirements of building materials are specified. A material or product in a given position must sustain acting forces, both natural and synthetic, that impact during its use period. The composition of the material or the synthetic product will chemically react or respond to the environment in which it is placed. Experience has shown that materials chemically react with one another and to the environment in which they are placed. Failure to observe and document this type of performance will cause valuable information for evaluating the performance of new synthetic products to be lost. Therefore, the final building material selection must take into account recorded research past experience, and test results.

Social and economic constraints placed on the client form another category of factors that must be evaluated when performance requirements are established for making material selections. Through history, various styles, trends, moral issues, and philosophies of life have all affected the client's ideas of what is socially acceptable in a living environment. Nonobservance of these points can be detrimental to material selection and product design. Economic constraints have become a highly sensitive concern for selecting building materials. In many cases, design professionals are restricted more by economics than by the actual performance criteria. The only way this imbalance of social and economic priorities can be handled successfully is for design professionals to identify all impact areas and then, working cooperatively with clients, assign relative values on each factor. Through a cooperative process, the client can become involved in making final design and product decisions. The design professional can no longer afford to estimate the client's opinions, situation in life, or social-economic constraints. Multiple variable requirements and impacts compel designers to work closely with clients during each stage of the decision-making process. To effectively manage technological change, information accumulation, energy constraints, material shortages, and other variables, a systems approach must involve the client and specialist in the decision-making team.

Environmental codes, standards, and building code requirements, set forth by state and federal legislation, establish constraints that impact on the final building material, design and selection process. These codes and standards set minimum requirements that provide for the health, safety, and welfare of the public. No design professional can work outside of these requirements. Because of certification and registration programs, design professionals are held accountable for all decisions for building design and material evaluation and selection. The future projects an ever-increasing number of responsibilities associated with building codes and standards. Building codes are based upon known physical limitations of the human body, which requires the designer to be aware of biological and technological factors, before safe building environments can be created. The best way to incorporate these considerations is to identify standards and codes that impact on design solutions within the community where the building is to be constructed. A systematic account of all codes, standards, and requirements will facilitate an effective design decision that provides for the health, safety, and welfare of the client. By using a systems approach to identify user needs, environmental factors, social-economic constraints, and environmental standards and building codes, design professionals can better establish a basis for building design and material selection decisions.

Identification of Performance Criteria

Performance requirements can correctly illustrate user needs, impacts, and constraints. The major goal is a fulfillment of the clients' needs, which are dependent upon properly stated performance requirements. Performance requirements must be identified and fulfilled on two levels: Level One: expected performance of a product or material; Level Two: expected performance of a total building system. Both levels of performance should be correlated with the clients' willingness to accept a predetermined level of risk. The final capability of a material or product can be observed in regard to its performance variables. The variables should be documented while the materials and products are responding to human and environmental factors. Clearly stated performance requirements and variables provide the basis for identifying performance criteria to evaluate and select materials and products. The performance criteria can be sorted into categories and levels so that is is possible to weigh the impact on material and product selection. The level of acceptable client risk will greatly influence the weighing of performance criteria.

Every design professional has a responsibility to work with clients before determining material and product selection to crystallize requirements. The collected information must be organized and rewritten into performance requirements which formulate the areas of concentration for making design and material selection decisions. Accurately defined performance criteria can guide the designer in systematically making a final judgement. The designer can then evaluate the final decision by criteria stated in the programming stage; double-checking and making sure that every area of impact has been considered.

If a library of information is developed, it will be possible to document performance criteria used in previous design programs. This information can then be referred to for solving new material selection problems. The process of documenting performance criteria should be considered part of a systematic approach to acquiring information. Steps and procedures should be established so that the design professional gathering information can follow a set procedure. Some guidelines for developing this procedure are as follows:

1.   Identify all present user needs that can be observed, researched and documented. Search for future demands or constraints that may have an impact on the client.

2.   Define all environmental conditions that impact on the materials and products used, the external environmental factors, as well as the internal environmental conditions, such as the function of the user in the facility and demands upon the client and employees. These implications should be incorporated into the final decision making process.

3.   Social, economic constraints placed upon the client, cultural, and community responsibilities subjected to, and anticipated reaction to demands are all situations relevant to the design professional's final decision. Economic planning will play a major role in establishing performance criteria based on material costs, maintenance, and user needs. It is important for design decisions to be based on well-defined social-economic impacts.

4.   All municipal, state, and federal laws that will have an impact on the building design and material or product selection can guide the

decision-making process to fulfill all health, safety, and welfare requirements of the user. Safety aspects of material performance and code fulfillment must be evaluated for changes in insurance ratings. In some cases greater savings can be incurred through the use of higher performance, quality materials having a better insurance rating because they have a higher endurance rating against fire, water, and temperature change.

5.   Technological capabilities must be considered prior to developing performance criteria. The design professional must consider human capabilities for fulfilling the requirements in the performance statements. Working outside the limits of technological capabilities will create major building material and product problems for members of the construction industry.

6.   Time and scheduling for the proper development and production of products have become important factors in the production industry. It is important to consider management and control measures. Steps must be taken in preparing performance criteria that insure product development and building material selection will fulfill the quality aspects desired by the client. A team approach to communication will help the development of effective performance criteria statements.

7.   Material evaluators and selectors should correlate established performance criteria with identified construction failures in order to generate steps toward avoiding future problems. Chart 18 pinpoints some of the design and construction stages where failures can occur.

CHART 18.   Stages Where Possible Failures Occur in the Development and Use of Products and Materials

1	Improper design
2	Lack of quality control during manufacturing
3	Incorrect application or installation
4	Improper continued use
5	Lack of maintenance

The professional responsible for product and material selection should be aware of each point of possible failure in product and material development and use. Control measures should be implemented at each crucial stage to reduce errors in product development and application. Quality-control programs instituted at each stage of development can prevent many design, production, and construction failures.

Weighting Performance Criteria

Once performance criteria have been identified, their relative importance will need to be evaluated. This can best be accomplished through a systematic weighting of each criterion. Through a weighting process, a hierarchial arrangement of performance criteria can be developed prior to the design decision. A thorough evaluation of user needs will identify areas of greatest impact. The areas found to be most critical to the final performance can be weighted according to the client's value rating. By weighting the performance criteria statements, the design professional can indicate the relative importance of functional, technological, physiological, sociological, economic, and other impacts according to client's observed and documented needs. The weighting system can be developed to use numerical values given to selected sets of performance criteria. By establishing a numerical value, both the design professional and the client can work together to formulate an effective performance criteria rating that will indicate areas that are most important to the client or user. A weighting system has many values:

1.   Allowing clients to interact with the design professional for stating concern about the final performance.
2.   Allowing the users (if different from clients) to contribute toward weighting the performance criteria.
3.   Provides the design professional with the type of information that will enable him to make an effective judgement based on prior research, experience, and other documented information.

4.   Provide background information that can be documented during the decision-making process for building material and product selection. Any deviations from established decisions can be documented and used as evidence in later periods of questioning and final performance studies.

5.   Provide documented information for the development of a library on building material and product selection. Once the building is in operation, documented information can be evaluated based on actual performance. A survey of the building components and their relative performance to the total structure can be documented and used as evidence and support in future building material selection programs.

6.   Provide the opportunity for design consultants and specialists to be brought into the decision-making process. The performance criteria statements can be made available to the other members of the building construction industry such as contractors, manufacturers, and others responsible for acting together to develop and evaluate the final materials and products. All team members will be given a chance to have input in the final decision-making process. They will be given an opportunity to agree upon the final selection as the best material or product to fulfill the identified performance requirements.

7.   Historic data banks of information generated in weighing performance criteria and building material selection can be developed by design professionals responsible for building design. Data banks will enable future design professionals to take advantage of documented information on the actual performance of materials and synthetic products. At present, there is not a central data bank that contains performance information that would support the design professional in making good judgements about the use of products and building materials. Only limited information is available from design professionals who have made an effort to document information on building performance.

The present material selection process is a very subjective one. By developing a weighting process for performance criteria and by information documentation, the design professional can be more objective. The technological means for storing and retrieving weighted performance criteria make it possible to work systematically with greater quantities of information during the final design decision. The use of the computer and other automated techniques for storing and retrieving information are now available at lower costs so that greater advantages in cost and time can be accrued by small and large organizations. The effectiveness of automation enables the design professional to be more prepared to solve client problems than in the past. To develop an objective selection process requires the establishment and fulfillment of the systematic steps identified in Chart 19.

CHART 19.   Critical Steps in the Product and Material Evaluation and Selection Process

1   Define need
2   Identify performance required
3   Establish evaluation criteria
4   Recall past performance variables
5   Identify choice of products and materials available
6   Acquire test results
7   Obtain field feedback
8   Develop product or material evaluation matrix

Use of a Matrix for Information Relationships

The complexity of information in the design field requires performance standards to be displayed in the form of a matrix to make accurate projections and design judgements. A matrix demonstrates graphically relations of products and materials to needs and goals. The graphic presentation of the interaction of criteria allows design professionals to direct clients attention to possible problem areas. It demonstrates requirements that should be evaluated specially due to the number of factors that affects final selection. Performance criteria should be identified and related to variables that may alter the material or product's performance. The frequency of interaction can be documented to illustrate areas the design professional should be especially concerned with. The most important areas of concern can be graphically shown to other members of the decision-making team taking part in the selection process.

The graphic matrix, developed in Chart 20 and shown in Chart 21, can present the design professional with a more accurate portrayal of

CHART 20. Developing a Building Material Evaluation Matrix

Step 1 Define the performance criteria to be used for evaluating a product or material. This information forms the left-hand column 1 of the evaluation matrix (see page 81 for identifying performance criteria).

Step 2 Provide left-hand column 2, adjacent to performance criteria listing, for listing the performance criteria weighting factors that are derived on the basis of the relative importance of each criterion for the use of material or product analyzed. These weights should be expressed in units of 100 (see page 84 for performance criteria weighting).

Step 3 Locate scientific and historic information sources on which findings can be weighted. These areas of evaluation information form the vertical objective rating column 1 and 2.

Step 4 Identify key people responsible for making design, construction evaluation, and selection decisions. These evaluators form vertical column 3.

Step 5 Specify the client and users responsible for establishing project and design objectives. These evaluators form vertical column 4.

Step 6 Separate columns for obtaining (1) objective score, (2) subjective score, (3) score influenced by Criteria Weighting Factor, (4) total scores, and (5) critical score rating.

Special Considerations

The identification of performance criteria, scientific, and historic information sources, design and construction decision makers, and the client/user should be made in accordance with the special requirements of each project. The design professional should be the leader for collecting and evaluating all relevant information. See page 88 and 89 for a sample form of a building material evaluation matrix and rating sheet.

CHART 21.   Building Material Evaluation Matrix and Rating Sheet

	EVALUATION AND WEIGHTING FACTORS								
	OBJECTIVE RATING								
Criteria Weighting Factor	Testing Laboratory	Field Tests	Established Standards	Building Codes	Past Performance	User Satisfaction	Time Frame of Performance	Observed Change in Material	Similarity of Future Use
Performance Criteria	Scientific Findings				Historic Findings				

Total Scores

CRITICAL SCORE RATING =

design factors. For example, a product being considered because of its fire endurance can be tested and correlated to the actual performance criteria established for the environment. Charts 22 and 23 explain how the matrix is used. As shown on Chart 24, roof insulation can be evaluated, and the design professional's rating of it entered on the matrix. Weaknesses in performance can be pinpointed so that the material

CHART 21.   (Continued)

Objec-tive Score	Archi-tect/ Engi-neer	Con-tractor	Man-ufac-turer	Con-sul-tants	Client	Users	Sub-jective Score	Score Influenced By Criteria Weighting Factor	TOTAL SCORES
EVALUATION AND WEIGHTING FACTORS									
	SUBJECTIVE RATING								
Score	Design/Const. Team				Owner		Scores		

or product composition can be changed to meet performance standards. This form of representation of problem areas provide an opportunity for other members of the construction industry to study the performance requirements. Manufacturers can easily be shown special requirements that must be fulfilled prior to product development as opposed to in the past when most material or product developers had little knowledge of the actual performance requirements. Through graphic techniques, levels of performance and responsibilities can be demonstrated. The design, construction, and manufacturing elements must work as a unified group of consultants and specialists to fulfill the common goal of developing a structure to satisfy the client's needs.

The matrix can be used to catalog past performance failures due to missing information or inadequate technology. Information and relationships on the matrix can be documented in databanks for future reference. Other design teams can utilize the research findings and evaluation records that document where the actual performance varied from the criteria.

The design professional's consultants and employees can use the information matrix to develop contract documents, such as working drawings and specifications. Draftsmen must be made aware of performance criteria and design parameters before design decisions are made. Material relationships established by working drawings and details sets the stage for success or failure of field performance. An inadequte material or product can cause a failure in the total system. Performance requirements must be related to all building components for the draftsmen to develop effective details on the working drawings.

The specifications as an integral part of contract documents must also be developed in accordance with the performance criteria. The failure to coordinate working drawings, specifications, and the final material or product selection may result in a construction failure in the total system. Designers are constantly faced with material or product decisions without knowing or having a program of performance requirements and criteria established for the project. A well-defined program statement and performance criteria for building materials and products can provide background information for designers and specifiers to make effective design decisions. The omission to translate user needs into a building program statement pertaining to functional elements of the building, can result in a failure on the part of the design professional to provide an adequate design solution to solve the client's needs. Most problems that occur in building performance are caused by poor communication or misunderstanding early in the design stages. Design professionals must take the time to identify performance requirements and criteria to improve a systematic evaluation and selection of building materials and products.

CHART 22.   Rating Key for Building Material Evaluation
Matrix and Rating Sheet

Degree of Satisfaction

8 = Excellent Satisfaction
7 = Good Satisfaction
6 = Average Satisfaction
5 = Moderate Satisfaction
4 = Poor Satisfaction
3 = No Satisfaction
2 = Very Unsatisfactory
1 = Totally incompatible
0 = No Relation
X = Unknown

Material Rating Equation*

$$\text{Material or Product rating} = \frac{A}{B}$$

A = Critical score rating
B = Number of performance criteria rated

Example: $52.36 = \dfrac{576}{11}$

Material or Product Rating = 52.36

*Taken from Building Material Evaluation Matrix and Rating Sheet Chart 25

CHART 23.   Using the Building Material Evaluation Matrix

Step 1   Design professional and client must first establish performance criteria weighting factors based on the relative importance of each criterion for the use of material or product analyzed. Each performance criteria factor should express the percent of increased emphasis. The percentage factors should total 100.

Step 2   The design team responsible for collecting evaluation information and weighting the scientific and historic findings form the objective rating columns. Special research and investigations are required to

Chart 23 (continued)

weight each performance criterion identified. Refer to rating key for the weighted value associated with a degree of satisfaction.

Step 3 Have each representative of the design and construction team evaluate the material or product and weight performance criteria fulfillment. These weightings form the subjective rating column which is based on (1) research, (2) observation, (3) past experience, and (4) personal judgements that enter into the decision making process. Refer to rating key for the weighted value associated with a degree of satisfaction.

Step 4 Have client and user evaluate the material or product and weight performance criteria fulfillment based on past experience and willingness to accept and approve the material or product under consideration.

Step 5 Obtain *scores* for the weightings in the objective and subjective rating columns.

Step 6 Modify the subjective score by multiplying it times the performance criteria weighting factor. This will reflect the design professionals' and clients' emphasis on each performance criteria identified.

Step 7 Add *scores* for objective and subjective columns to obtain a *total score* for each performance criterion evaluated.

Step 8 Add *total score* for each performance criterion to obtain a material or product *critical score rating*. The *critical score* rating will be considered as *A* in the equation for determining a material or product rating. Separate *critical score ratings* can be obtained for objective and subjective ratings.

Step 9 Total the number of performance criteria rated. This number will be considered as *B* in the rating equation.

Step 10 Determine the building *material or product rating* by using the following equation:

$$
\text{Material or Product rating} = \frac{A}{B} = \begin{array}{l} \text{Critical score rating} \\ \text{Number of performance} \\ \text{criteria rated} \end{array}
$$

CHART 24. Building Material Evaluation

Roof insulation

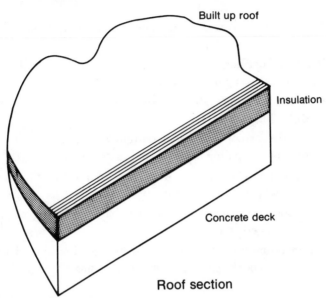

Built up roof

Insulation

Concrete deck

Roof section

Performance requirement

Roofing insulation should prevent heat passage and remain in a stable position so as to maintain bond between roof deck and roofing felts.

Performance Criteria

Insulation with an R value of 15 and a coefficient of lineal expansion of 0.0003 lin/ft. will resist heat passage and thermal movement.

Test Result for Brand X

R value = 10

Coefficient of lineal expansion = 0.200 lin/ft.

Evaluation

Results of research studies and tests show that this material is deficient in both resistance to heat flow and in thermal stability.

Design Professional's Judgement Rating

4 = Poor Satisfaction

The numerical results of building material evaluation should be entered on building material evaluation matrix and rating sheet—Chart 25.

Building Material Evaluation Matrix Capabilities

- A method to compare different materials and products on a numerical basis.
- It gives the decision maker an opportunity to systematically evaluate all major issues before making a choice.
- An opportunity to weight different performance criteria, identified needs, and limitations.
- It gives the decision maker an opportunity to evaluate a material or product by comparing objective and subjective weightings.
- An opportunity to compare weightings from different testing, research, and personal experience.
- An opportunity to make final selections based on findings and analysis of many criteria.
- An opportunity to make final selections based on objective or a combination of objective and subjective findings.

A Manual or Computerized Evaluation Matrix

A manual approach for an evaluation matrix will allow the user to refine performance criteria and techniques before selecting the best approach. Once a systematic approach has been established, it is then possible to store and retrieve performance requirements, variables, and criteria in a Computerized Evaluation Matrix. Criteria weighting by a numerical system will allow manipulation of a greater variety of information in the final evaluation process. Information handling and word processing systems now provide the capabilities for storing and retrieving valuable data in material and product evaluation programs. New communications systems that combine the use of the computer, a screen (CRT), and keyboard will provide the design professional with up-to-date technical literature on products and materials. Performance requirements and criteria can thus be projected and maniuplated for analysis, evaluation, and selection. These systems and programs enables the development of effective data banks containing material and product information as well as field performance recors. By structuring in-house design programs and systems to take advantage of stored information and the latest communication equipment, the design professional can become more responsive to future client needs.

Benefits of a Computer Program for Material Product Evaluation and Selection

- Time savings in data collection and searching.
- Standardization of input and output of information.
- Larger amounts of material performance information can be stored.
- Reduced errors in decision making.
- Provides a historic base for decision making.

CHART 25. Building Material Evaluation Matrix and Rating Sheet

| | | EVALUATION AND WEIGHTING FACTORS | | | | | | | | |
| | | OBJECTIVE RATING | | | | | | | | |
Performance Criteria	Criteria Weighting Factor	Testing Laboratory	Field Tests	Established Standards	Building Codes	Past Performance	User Satisfaction	Time Frame of Performance	Observed Change in Material	Similarity of Future Use
		Scientific Findings				Historic Findings				
Structural Serviceability	1.05	6	5	3	1	2	4	0	6	8
Fire Safety	1.05	2	1	6	8	4	3	2	1	6
Habitability	1.05	4	5	6	2	1	0	4	3	2
Durability	1.05	2	1	0	3	4	2	1	0	1
Practicability	1.05	8	7	6	3	0	1	2	4	6
Compatability	1.05	7	4	3	2	1	6	4	8	5
Maintainability	1.30	4	3	2	1	8	1	6	4	3
Code Acceptability	1.10	2	0	1	4	3	2	7	5	4
Economics	1.05	4	6	3	2	1	0	2	5	4
Material Availability	1.05	1	0	2	3	1	2	1		
Functionalism	1.20	7	8	2	1	0	1	5	6	3
Total Scores		47	40	34	30	25	25	37	42	43

CRITICAL SCORE RATING =

CHART 25. (Continued)

	EVALUATION AND WEIGHTING FACTORS								
	SUBJECTIVE RATING								
Objective Score	Architect/ Engineer	Contractor	Manufacturer	Consultants	Client	Users	Subjective Score	Score Influenced By Criteria Weighting Factor	TOTAL SCORES
Score	Design/Const. Team				Owner			Scores	
35	2	6	X	8	4	1	21	22.05	57.05
33	0	5	2	7	8	3	25	26.25	59.25
27	1	3	7	3	5	0	19	19.95	46.95
14	5	8	1	5	7	6	32	33.6	47.6
37	2	7	X	8	0	1	18	18.9	55.9
40	6	X	8	5	3	2	24	25.2	65.2
32	0	1	3	X	2	4	10	13.0	45.0
28	8	4	5	1	8	7	33	36.3	64.3
25	3	7	5	8	1	3	27	28.35	53.35
19	X	3	0	4	X	5	12	12.6	31.6
33	7	2	4	0	1	X	14	16.8	49.8
323	34	46	35	49	39	32	235	253	576
									576

2.4

Responsibilities of the Design Professional

Client Expectations

Clients are placing greater demands on the design professional than ever before because of the complexity of the technological world, and task responsibilities in the working environment. Public demands cause businesses to be more responsive to customers' desires. Space needs require design professionals to create building environments to fulfill more complex user requirements. Product demands are now exceedingly great because of economic pressures on both the producer and consumer. In the commercial and industrial world, working environments must support activities between departments, people, and machines. To design supportive work environments requires detailed user need programs and a systematic approach to the design process.

Contemporary clients expect to work with a design professional who is highly trained in building technology, materials, performance, interrelationships, and structural capabilities. Clients expect the designer to be able to individually interpret client ideas, and fulfill all design requests without error. Most clients do not consider the design professional in terms of human limitations, either educational or by experience. Design professionals are not able to predict varying capabilities of the contractor, manufacturer, and other team members. Working relationships where the manufacturer and contractor are separated from the design team make it difficult for the design professional to be accountable for the total building structure and its component parts. Yet, clients view design professionals as decisive members of the design team who have control over every other member of the team, and activity associated with project construction.

Every step and decision of the design professional's should be carried out systematically based on accurate information. A truly effective design professional works with the client, studies user needs, and then establishes performance criteria and incorporates the experience of the building design team. The professional approach to design begins with an effective contract. The design professional can build confidence by organizing the design program and establishing the responsibilities of each team member. Objective planning on the part of the design professional will help fulfill the clients' expectations.

Professional Responsibilities

Once a design professional has become registered, he has accepted the responsibility of carrying out his design performance to the best of his ability and stated that all state and federal laws and standards will be fulfilled. He has taken a personal oath to work with the tools, knowledge, and experience that he has acquired in architectural design and building construction. As a design professional, he is entrusted with using the best of judgement at all times. He is expected to make decisions based on a systematic organization of all known information. Designers who operate systematically, respond in good faith, and perform each task in a competent manner, build strong professional images while effectively responding to client requests.

A record of successful design decisions is indicative of a person's ability to organize information and make effective judgements. Design professionals who take the time to systematically organize information and identify performance criteria establish a basis for making accurate judgements. Recent legal cases have shown that when the design professional operates competently, by documenting all findings, utilizing contemporary work of other design professionals, and operating in a

conventional manner, he is judged to be performing in the best professional manner. In most of these legal cases, the design professional has
been acquitted of operating negligently and as a result, has not incurred financial losses.

The future promises only greater problems in design, construction, and
manufacturing activities with a corresponding increase in the number
of responsibilities associated with building technology and design. For
the design professional to manage the increased pressures and still remain responsive to the needs of clients, he will need to systematically
develop a process for building material evaluation and selection. The
design professional can thus demonstrate to his client that he is prepared to manage complex building problems, economically. A systems
approach to design, information gathering, and research enables the
decision making team to more effectively solve the clients' problems.
Decision making in future building programs requires the design professional to work cooperatively with other experienced members of the
construction industry. It will be the design professional's responsibility
to organize the most responsive and effective team. The design professional that operates in a systematic manner that is truly responsive to
the client's demands will undoubtedly be the most successful.

Team Work Requirements

With an ever-increasing complexity in building technology, designers
will become more dependent upon other specialists and consultants
who can provide the type of information needed for making good
building material evaluation and selection judgements. This decision
making process can successfully be accomplished if the design professional performs three major team work activities effectively.

1. *Communication.*   It is important to communicate in every step of
the design decision process. Problems with existing building material
performance should be discussed and new information for available
products and buildings materials obtained and evaluated. The design

professional should take every opportunity to discuss the problems in material performance with other members of his profession. Once a decision is made, every phase of design implementation with the manufacturer and the contractor must be discussed, so there can be no question as to what areas should be explored further to eliminate potential failures. Communication will serve as the key activity which will unite all members of the building team.

2. *Cooperation.* To be responsive as a building team, the designer, manufacturer, and contractor must develop a systematic approach for cooperating effectively during each step of the decision making process. Once performance criteria have been studied, and acceptance has been given by each team member, those responsible can work together to carry out the development activities to fulfill final performance requirements. Cooperation must begin at the very early stages of the decision-making process, and into the final construction phase of building design. If problems arise and studies are required to make a design decision, it will become the responsibility of the total team to decide on which steps must be taken to eliminate or solve the problems in the best interest of the client. In many cases, a lack of coordination and cooperation has resulted in design and construction problems.

3. *Coordination.* It is important to develop a procedural plan that can be carried out by each member of the building design team. No member of the building team can afford to work independently or make decisions without relating to a team plan. Past experience has shown that good coordination can save everyone time and money, and result in the production of high-quality materials and products that satisfy client's needs. Recent breakdowns in the construction industry have shown that many times it is simply a lack of coordination that caused some discipline in the design or construction team to fail to interact at the proper time. Acting out of sequence can create major problems in design and construction programs. This can cause building components and systems to fail in the initial stages of building design and construction.

Communication, cooperation, and coordination have an impact upon building material performance. Failure to carry out any one of these activities can result in the misuse of products and materials. A lack of communication between the design professional and product manufacturer can result in a misunderstanding of performance criteria established for fulfilling user needs. Each stage of product development and installation is dependent upon communication, coordination, and cooperation if effective performance is to be achieved. The important point is to recognize that team work requirements in transferring information are essential to achieving the expected material or product performance.

Future Role of Design Professionals

Forecasts in building design and construction predict material shortages, energy and economic crises, changing technologies, and more complex work responsibilities. These impacts will force the design profession to develop better methods of making design decisions. Specialists in building technology and material research can help design professionals develop effective solutions to design problems. Attempts to work independently from other disciplines have created problems and failed to provide an effective design service.

Some of the team members in building design that work with building materials and products every day are the architect, engineer, interior designer, planner, specifier, manufacturer, contractor, and building inspector. All these team members and building material researchers gather information constantly. Yet very little documented information is available for their findings. If each design professional were responsible for documenting field problems, an exceptional library of information of how building materials and products perform in particular applications could be constructed. Since this type of information is not available, only past and limited experience can be utilized. This is a very weak basis on which to make building material selections. As design professionals encounter greater complexities in product and material development, they will need to take advantage of performance monitoring, research information, and product research to find answers to problems. By understanding how materials and products have performed under past conditions, the selection process will be able to be improved.

Design professionals working in every area of building construction will need to document valuable findings so that they can be utilized by others. Past weaknesses in information documentation and retrieval have allowed different disciplines in the construction industry to make decisions without important and necessary information. The information might have existed in some other fields' research files but due to a lack of communication it has failed to be accessible to a decision maker. The isolated and uncoordinated working positions of each discipline is one of the major drawbacks to communicating daily construction experiences. An information exchange system that allows disciplines to have access to, and benefit from others experiences can only benefit the professional responsible for design decisions.

A new era in communication technology is in the offing that can make information storage and retrieval a more efficient process. The development of a universally accepted construction language could assist the building industry in organizing a comprehensive Construction Information System. Efficient exchange and use of information will be hampered until design professionals work together in the development of a large-scale information system. Future design, building material evaluation, and selection programs will be dependent upon organized data banks. Existing construction-related information systems already provide valuable information for decision making. However very few professionals take advantage of these systems.

Legal Responsibilties

Greater legal responsibilities are being placed upon design professionals working with complex construction problems. Every act and decision of the professional is a potential error. A design professional's judgements are so varied and broad in scope that it is easy to see where failures occur because the proper information was not used for developing the final solution. When this happens, the design professional is regarded as having acted negligently. There are many cases where courts have judged design professionals to have acted negligently and have been found guilty of nonperformance due to unsubstantiated design judgements. A design generalist charged with many responsibilities will be unable to withstand the legal pressures if the experience and knowledge of specialists, consultants, and other members of the team are not incorporated into his practice. It now is a personal responsibility of every design professional to seek the proper support and information for making design judgements. It is very important for the design professional to consult with specialists who can provide the proper information on material and product performance. If this is done and the statements and literature that were made available are documented, sound bases of information for making decisions and experience will be built. A continued relationship with the building team will insure that the product or material was developed and installed according to specifications. The design professional who has carried out a systematic approach to define the performance criteria and has worked with other team members to evaluate impacts, will be in the best position to make effective design judgements.

The design professional who identifies where specialists and the design team interact is admitting in a competent manner his limitations in judgement. This will demonstrate in a court of law that the designer has acted responsibly in performing his tasks by integrating the experience of specialists into the decision-making process. Several building material failures have shown that some design professionals have not performed in a systematic manner, because they did not regard the experience of other members of the building team. Positive examples can also be shown where design professionals have worked systematically and have successfully acted competently by using the following procedures:

1. Material and product technical information was gathered and was evaluated against performance criteria.

2. The product or building material representative was called, and questions regarding its capability to perform as identified on performance statements were addressed.
3. The material or product representative was present during the installation of the material to check its relationship to other building components.

When the design professional has taken these three major precautions, he is showing that he is not making judgements beyond his capability. Accurate judgements on the performance of other people are almost impossible to make because there is no way an individual can predict or promise how other people will perform. This illustrates the tremendous need for interacting and cooperating with all disciplines in the construction industry that impact on the final product. A sharing of responsibilities, either directly or indirectly, through a contract is essential for making the best design decisions. The success of the design profession is dependent upon new contractual relationships that encourage different disciplines to work cooperatively. Design professionals that cooperate and share responsibilities strengthen their own disciplines' decision-making process as well as in other organizations associated with the construction industry. An organized building design and construction team has the potential to make more effective decisions and be more responsive to client needs.

The legal implications of recent court cases have demonstrated that the design professional is acting as a seller of the product and under the present law, the seller shares much greater responsibilities than he did many years ago. It is now the buyer who is demanding that the product perform as is described or identified in the program. If the product does not perform as was called for in the performance requirements, the client has the legal right to request fulfillment of those areas of nonperformance. When this occurs, the design professional is held accountable for nonperformance of a building material or product or a total building system. Once this happens, the design professional is on his own and must be able to account for all the judgements that were made prior to the design decision. If he is unable to supply the proper information, he can be held negligent. As the law changes, there will undoubtedly be new problems developing as a result of greater responsibilities being shared by all members of the design team. This is why it is very important to develop strong lines of communication, cooperation, and coordination, so that for the benefit of every discipline, responsibilities can be shared and the type of performance that is expected by clients can be achieved. If the profession fails to do this, there is no question that it should be held accountable.

2.5

Use of a Systematic Approach

Application of a Systematic Approach by the Building Design Team

Every person responsible in the decision-making process must be alerted to all of the important stages in the design process. The importance of incorporating past experiences at the right time must be apparent to the design professional responsible for making decisions. Each member of the team must understand the language and management constraints that are part of the systematic approach for problem solving. The building material selection process should be treated just as importantly as any of the other design decisions.

Effective procedures and guidelines must be established for each decision maker. A systematic approach to the building material selection process can provide the framework for collecting documented information, research findings, and experiences by all members of the building design team. Through the use of an interaction matrix, decision makers can identify performance criteria and pinpoint problem areas that need primary attention. An interaction network for information identification, retrieval, and utilization can provide the organization for effective decision making.

The complexity of user needs and environmental, social, and economic factors requires a systems approach to successfully organize and evaluate problem variables. By establishing a common ground for communication, team members will be better able to cooperate in pre paring solutions to structured design problems. The matrix of impact variables and performance criteria provides a more efficient means for evaluating and selecting building materials. Every member of the decision-making team needs to understand user needs, design parameters, and projected goals before making final decisions. Only through a common understanding of user needs, will the design professionals and their consultants be able to work together in solving the clients' problems. A systematic approach to the building product and material evaluation and selection process provides a basis for better communication and successful decision making. It forces the evaluation and selection process to "dig deeper" to go beyond the cursory considerations normally taken into account by decision makers. The following example highlights three selection considerations that serve to illustrate the complexity and importance of the systematic approach to product and material selection.

Exploring the Evaluation and Selection Options

A client is involved in making a selection of acoustical ceiling tile for a multipurpose room in an elementary school. The designer has indicated some of the possible material choices such as wood fiber tile, mineral tile, metal pan tile, etc. In the selection process, only three of the many performance criteria are identified:

1. Economics.
2. Fire safety.
3. Acoustical rating.

Several other performance criteria that should be considered, such as code acceptability, will not be dealt with in this example. From the preliminary evaluation of the three performance criteria it is taken for granted that the cheaper tile is going to be the most economical and therefore the best selection. However, if this decision is analyzed more carefully and a more systematic evaluation is conducted, the tradeoffs shown in Chart 26 will be discovered.

A fire insurance study of the elementary school plans and proposed materials will provide valuable information for a cost analysis of alternative material choices. If the elementary school under consideration is valued at $2,000,000 and contains a multipurpose room 30 x 70 ft with a proposed wood fiber acoustical ceiling as compared to a mineral tile, it would produce the following economic tradeoffs over a 1 year period.

CHART 26.   Product Attributes

Acoustical Tile	Sound Absorption Rating	Flame Spread Rating	System Cost per sq./ft
Wood fiber	NRC = 45–65 STC = not available	75–150	$1.00–$1.25
Mineral	NRC = 70–80 STC = 45–49	10–25	$1.35–$1.50
Metal pan and fiberglass	NRC = 70–90 STC = 10	5	$2.25–$2.75

Note: The numbers used in the chart are approximate and illustrate evaluation relationships

Acoustical Tile Wood Fiber. Insurance premiums would be increased as a result of a flame spread rating 75–150 greater than 25. The additional charge will be incurred at a rate of 3¢ per $100 of assessed value (80% market value) per year. Insurance premium increase = 2,000,000 x 80% = $1,600,000 = 16,000 x 0.03 = $480.00 per year additional charge.

Mineral Tile. Mineral tile costs 23¢ per sq. ft more than wood fiber tile = area 30 x 70 ft = 2100 sq. ft x 0.23 = $483.00 additional initial cost.

The increased initial cost of selecting a mineral tile which satisfies a greater number of performance criteria turns out to be also equivalent to the additional insurance premiums incurred by selecting the cheaper wood fiber tile.

The systematic evaluation process discovers that building fire insurance will be substantially increased as a result of selecting a wood fiber tile with a flame spread rating of 75–150. According to insurance ratings for building materials, when the flame spread rating goes above 25 an additional charge is incurred with an increase in the overall insurance premium for the entire facility. This charge can add several cents per hundred dollars of assessed value per year. On a large facility the additional charge, based on current insurance ratings, could far exceed the initial savings incurred in the purchase price. Therefore, an in-depth systematic evaluation procedure is recommended to discover critical tradeoffs that relate overall performance to greatest value. Product and material analysis programs such as value engineering and life-cycle costing should be utilized to derive evaluation data for the selection matrix.

Design professionals will be able to effectively utilize the systematic approach to building materials and products in the following design and evaluation stages:

Stage One. Design Professional and Client Interaction

The first and most sensitive stage of design is when the design professional and client discuss the uses of building materials and products. In the early stages of architectural planning, the client must be made aware of the benefits of systematically identifying and utilizing research information and past experience for making building material selections. The design professional should identify user needs, performance requirements of building materials, maintenance considerations, and other factors important for developing a good building design program. The use of a systematic approach can demonstrate to the client factors that must be analyzed in the building design process. The client can have input in building material and product evaluation and selection by structuring the design program and the decision-making process.

Stage Two. Design Professional and Consultant Interaction

After initial client discussions have determined user needs, the design professional must then interact with his consultants. At this time the design professional will want to convey to the selected consultants their responsibilities for making decisions that affect the final solution to the client's requests. Every consultant should thoroughly understand the constraints under which the design professional is working. Each consultant should be aware of the design constraints and be able to make usuable decisions regarding building material and product selection. The ultimate goal is to systematically fulfill the performance requirements described in the design program. Everyone must be responsible for the goal that was presented to the design professional by his client. Each member of the design consulting team should follow the project performance criteria. The list of performance criteria produced by the design professional can be distributed to the consulting team as a checklist for making building material selection decisions and design details. The checklist of performance requirements and criteria highlight the responsibilities that a professional must share with the entire design team. Each design team decision can then be documented and related to the performance criteria and standards set by the design professional for evaluation later in the construction process.

Stage Three. Design Professional and His Design Team

Like consultants, members of the building design team are part of the design professional's organization responsible for performance criteria that must be fulfilled. Each member of the team must be given the same set of directives and guidelines for making design decisions. A library of information of research findings, material performance, evaluations, and experience, provide support for the final decision-making process. A systematic manner of utilizing material and product information will save time in the programming and building design phases. Each design professional can thus evaluate the project by using the performance criteria established. A systems approach will create more team cooperation and coordination during all stages of building design and construction.

Stage Four.   Design Professional and Specifier

The working relationship the design professional establishes with the specification consultant is critical to the building design and material selection process. During material selection, the person in charge of preparing building specifications becomes responsible for fulfilling the established performance criteria also. The design professional must communicate to the specifier the constraints taken into account prior to developing a facility for the client. The specifier can use the best judgement and design experience for carrying out the building material and product selection process only through a thorough understanding of the common goals and responsibilities. If a systematic approach is used and performance criteria have been established, the specifier can conduct the necessary research to make effective decisions about the products and materials that will satisfy the needs identified in the initial design program. The specifier must have all the possible documented information and research findings available so that when the formal specification is prepared, it is clearly understood what responsibilities are shared by every member of the building design and construction team. Personal liabilities must be clarified so the manufacturer and the contractor have a sharp awareness of the performance levels that are expected by the design professional and client. A lack of communication during this stage can cause a total failure of performance in the design solution.

Specifiers are an important link in the chain of communication that connects the design team. They serve a liaison function at times between the design professional, consultants, and other employees responsible for putting together the total contract document. Specifiers can locate the areas of information that must be gathered and what decision points must be established with a systematic approach to dealing with building materials and product performance criteria to fulfill the original intent of the design program. They will collect past experiences, research, and documented information in the design library of building performance evaluation records. Past research and performance records enable the specifier to make logical and objective design decisions.

Stage Five. Design Professional and the Drafting Team

The drafting team is constantly in a position to make design judgements while developing working drawing details and preparing the final construction documents. Without a set of directives, the guideposts for making design judgements are lacking. With a well-defined set of selection criteria, the drafters can work under the same constraints that affect the building design team. Without a checklist of critical decision making steps identified, judgements will be made without realizing that some may cause a variance in the original intended performance of a building material. Through an established set of performance criteria, the drafters can fully understand the importance of judgements and the final design solutions' impact upon the final process. The performance criteria should be cataloged under a numbering system that relates to a library of information regarding a particular material or product. Through this process, the common goal of structuring a successful building material and product relationship will be fulfilled and can serve as an excellent means for expanding the employee's knowledge of building design information.

Stage Six. Design Professional Interaction with Manufacturer and Contractor

When the design professional decides to work with a particular product or building material, it is important to meet with experienced individuals who have dealt with the material or product on a daily basis. The manufacturer's representative is someone who has first-hand knowledge of the building product and how it performed in past facilities. The representative's records should demonstrate that the product or material can perform as requested in the performance criteria set forth by the design professional. Compliance with established performance criteria should be documented for the purpose of making future design and building material selection decisions. During this preliminary review, the manufacturer or representative should be given the performance criteria that must be fulfilled by their product. If this cannot be accomplished through the development of the product or material, the manufacturer can have input into structuring performance requirements and criteria that might still allow their product to be considered. A clear understanding must be established before either party can proceed to make final decisions in the building design process.

The contractor's experience should be used to contribute support to the final building material selection process. In most cases, contractors are not given an opportunity to express their experiences and findings at the early stages in the design decision making process. These personal experiences could give tremendous support to the design professional who is lacking the field experience that only the contractor might contribute. Only through a systematic approach of identifying performance criteria can the decision makers establish an effective process for making successful design decisions. The contractor might be able to suggest areas that could cause later problems. These clues will enable the design professional, specifier, manufacturer, and all other members of the building construction team to make more effective building material selections. A logical and systematic approach to communicating and collecting all valuable information is highly necessary for the final design and building material selection process. The design professional cannot work in isolation but must take advantage of all the known information from experience, research, or documented findings.

Stage Seven. Project Evaluation Before and During Construction

Upon completion of the contract documents, the design professional and client can review projects using the selection and performance criteria as a guide to a final acceptance of the design solution. Material usage can be justified by documented performance statements that were prepared by each member of the building team during the design stages. Documentation of all judgements and decisions assists both the client and the design professional in establishing better communication lines during the final building construction stages. The design professional, can document the acceptance of the client at this point as well as indicate the clients' understanding of the final solution that was prepared. Variations can be made by reevaluating the performance criteria and their importance as related to user needs established in the architectural programming stage.

Later changes and substitutions can be compared to earlier decisions by reviewing requirements and evaluating their relation to the design criteria. Once construction is begun, the final performance evaluation program can also begin. Materials can be observed as they perform within the environment. At this time field performance feedback programs are important for defining performance information that is needed to support future building material and design decisions to be made by the design professional. After construction is completed, the material can be evaluated as it performs in relationship to all the other products and materials used in the project. Records of the actual building material performance give the design professional the most valuable information for making future building materials selections.

Stage Eight. Building Performance Evaluation

Through the use of the systematic material selection process, the designer can monitor the performance of each material and product that has been selected for the project. Variations can be compared to the estimated performance at the time of building design. The initial selection criteria and final evaluation can serve as a basis for developing an effective feedback process. Information recorded during the design process can be used by the design team on future building projects. The process of satisfying all performance criteria in the decision-making process and the evaluation of field performance can assist information identification and collection for future building design problems.

Memos should be written on all material performance in the field. These memos can then be placed in performance criteria files and used as reference materials. A retrieval system can be the office's system for selecting relevant information for each design program established in the organization. Each team member can have access to the documented information and use the retrieval system to recover valuable findings many years after the building was constructed.

Client Input and Responsibility

Performance criteria specified for all major building materials and products, make it easier for the client to have input in the decision-making process during any stage of the building design program. The client usually does not play a major role in any of the decision-making programs, but simply gives the final acceptance which is based on limited information and a set of working drawings that may be difficult for the client to understand and interpret. The design professional should be responsible to structure a systematic program that allows the client to interact at any stage in the design process. This will allow clients to portray their feelings and needs during the design process. These ideas and needs sometimes change or may become crystallized after working along with the design professional.

It is more effective for decision makers to evaluate information if experience and research contribute to the body of knowledge needed to make the final judgement about a building material or product. When the building team and client begin to work on a project, many personal experiences can be discussed and evaluated before making a final decision. By setting up the mechanism to incorporate ideas and experiences as the design solution is developed, the final decision makers can take advantage of all of the available information. If the framework for clients to interact effectively at various stages in the decision-making process is provided, they will feel a part of the program and feel a responsibility for the final solution to the problem. This kind of working relationship will improve communication during the building design and construction process.

Bringing clients into the decision-making process will allow them to establish priorities that they feel are important according to demands that are placed upon them. An objective approach can then be taken in the final decision-making process. As priorities are established, the weighting system for the performance criteria should be developed so that performance issues can be successfully evaluated. A numerical weighting system will enable the design professional to establish priorities by obtaining valuable client input at the outset of the building design program. A matrix of performance criteria and priorities with weights should be developed (pages 96 and 97) and presented to clients. This will enable the clients to see their contribution to the design process and their responsibility for projecting needs, financial limitations, and other constraints that will have impact on the decision-making process. Many clients have employees who should also contribute user information to the design professional. Through the use of an evaluation matrix, both client and employees can provide vital information from experiences to carry out more efficient job responsibilities in production and management.

A systematic approach to the building design process can guide the design professional in searching for good information and experience records. Clients and their representatives can be tremendous resources for defining design requirements and weighting performance criteria. Only by developing a systematic approach that provides for multidisciplinary interaction can one take advantage of all documented findings and experience. Past experience has shown that design professionals working in isolation create design problems and misunderstandings that have resulted in tremendous legal suits. The design professional must consider all possible ways of organizing and systematically incorporating the ideas of many different disciplines that affect the building, design, and construction process. The future success of a building environment will be very much dependent upon team coordination, cooperation, and communication. No one individual will be able to act as the master builder of many centuries ago.

Management and Organization of Information

A systematic approach to the identification of building performance and material performance criteria will allow the designer to structure an effective information documentation system. The performance criteria associated with each product and material can be identified through a numbering and lettering system that documents field feedback, research information, experiences, and any other relevant information that will support the designer in the final decision making process. Once the material has been documented, it can serve all members of the building design team. It can also be used in developing in-house education programs. These programs can serve as employee-training programs for developing the expertise to improve the material evaluation and selection process.

Recorded field experiences and research findings can be used to improve the effectiveness training of new employees responsible for making successful building material and product selections. The knowledge acquired by people who have had many years of experience has not been shared in the past. Many specialists have worked years and gained a great deal of experience in the material performance areas, and yet have never been able to donate this information. By using effective documentation techniques over a period of time, a library of technical information to serve people entering the design profession can be developed. A good information system will allow the design field to build upon the past experiences of others and no longer make the same mistakes while investing less time and money in making design decisions.

Design professionals are now paying the penalty of spending greater amounts of time and monies researching and proving the performance of materials that have been in existence for many years. Through an effective management and information program, every office practicing in the design field could take advantage of the experiences being gained by members of the construction industry on a world-wide basis. Building research stations around the world are continually researching new materials and products. If this information were systematically recorded, indexed, and stored, it could be retrieved for use by every design professional and client involved in the decision-making process. New information systems have now made it possible to develop effective libraries of technical data on building material selection and performance. Communication stations consisting of a computer terminal, cathode ray tube, and keyboard will provide instant access to valuable construction information. Product material evaluators will be able to manipulate data instantaneously during the design process. Effective data banks will greatly improve the efficiency of the product and material evaluation process.

Legal Implications of Using a Systematic Approach

Legal problems due to product and material failures have been increasing over the past several years. These problems are the result of factors such as the complexity of building materials, products, and the number of people involved in design, manufacturing, and construction. The complexity of the many problems associated with material selection can only be coped with when individuals responsible for making decisions share the responsibilities of the building design and construction industry.

Recent court cases involving material product failures have demonstrated the advantage of having information available and documented for proving the competency of the performance of the decision makers. Cases that have demonstrated a poorly developed design solution, and a lack of communication with all team members, have usually found the design professional also responsible for negligent acts. If court cases involving material and building failures are analyzed, it can be seen which responsibilities need to be fulfilled in the early stages of the building design decision-making process. It is important to understand those acts that a design professional can and should perform when given the responsibility for making an effective design decision. Through the identification of performance criteria, material research findings, and performance records the design professional can identify priorities and alternatives for demonstrating that a sound and logical approach in the decision-making process has been taken. The design professional's first responsibility is to effectively work with everyone involved in the decision-making process. Each team member carries a personal responsibility for communication, coordination, and cooperation. If the design professional has made reasonable efforts to develop an objective and logical approach for working with fellow team members and clients, he or she will be judged as working competently with the techniques of this profession.

The courts' expectations of the design professional are no greater than what can be expected of the profession responding to the needs of the clients. Performance must be competent and carried out systematically using all available knowledge and professional methods. If the design professional uses good judgement in an objective manner and performs all responsibilities in a systematic way, he or she will be in the best position to substantiate all decisions. Evidence is necessary to demonstrate to other individuals what process was used and the thinking and judgements that brought the design professional to perform in a given manner. Many of the causes of building material failures have originated in the design professional's judgements made during the early decision-making process of building design. The problems actually stem from a lack of knowledge or inability to apply the most effective information at the right time to arrive at a reasonable decision. The only way the design professional can surmount the human weakness of simple forgetfulness or hasty decisions is through the use of a systematic approach to documenting and recalling information. Support for using a systematic approach becomes apparent when we see the vast areas of potential failure due to the lack of information or experience that are needed to make effective design decisions.

Through the establishment of performance criteria for evaluating and selecting building materials, all decisions the design professional makes when competently carrying out the responsibilities associated with his commission can be recorded. By clearly stating all performance requirements, issues that require further exploration and special expertise to obtain accurate information can be identified. A systematic approach forces the design professional to ask others to share their experience. This approach also serves as a mechanism for highlighting the timing for communication, cooperation, and coordination with other consultants and team members.

The most important point to establish is that the design professional used reasonable care and judgement to investigate all performance aspects of the products and materials. A matrix of performance criteria allows the design professional to record and maintain historic data on the performance of products and materials. The documented information can serve as records of past performance and predict areas of future performance or weaknesses. This information will establish proof that a systematic approach to investigate the product's reliability was taken.

The best building material performance information that the design professional can provide is documented historic performance data. Being able to show clients how a material or product performed under similar conditions is important during the evaluation and selection process. The client and user can be shown areas where risk is involved and where a product's ability to perform according to established performance criteria may be questionable.

Severe risk areas can be located by the matrix of performance criteria. These are areas where the client should be brought into the decision-making process. If the client chooses to take certain risks, the design professional can document all decisions and determine the high-risk areas on the performance matrix. When variations occur in the field performance of materials and products, it will be then easier to identify the responsible party or show the occurrence was beyond human control.

A systematic approach will enable the design professional to develop a design program for obtaining information related to the performance criteria of building materials and products. Some of the ways a systematic approach can help are as follows:

1. Better Coordination with Manufacturer

A systematic listing of performance criteria allows the design professional to work directly with the manufacturer to define the major areas of performance that must be fulfilled by the product or material. Once the guidelines have been established, the manufacturer can state the possibility of selected materials and products being able to perform in the requested manner. With a set of performance criteria, both manufacturers and design professionals can effectively communicate problem areas that must be overcome to satisfy the user's needs.

2. Evaluation of Past Performance

By using the established performance criteria, the design professional can obtain from the manufacturer a listing of similar applications of products or materials for evaluating past performance. Both the design professional and manufacturing representative can undertake a building materials evaluation program to identify the product's past performance. The manufacturer may have recorded information that pertains to the performance criteria matrix. Research by the design professional and manufacturer can be conducted in areas where little performance information is available. A systematic approach will allow both the design professional and manufacturing representatives to document every step in the decision-making process. This approach will provide the design professional an opportunity to look at all the variations and possible conditions under which the product was used, and who was responsible for the installation. Having identified performance criteria will establish a basis for the design professional to evaluate the actual performance of selected materials and products in constructed buildings and develop a resource library of performance information.

3. Compliance with Identified Performance Criteria

The material and product manufacturer should comply with the established performance criteria and furnish a guarantee or warranty, and statements of compliance. This information will provide the design professional with a record of the manufacturer's response to the established criteria for specified products or materials. It is valuable to obtain a written statement of how the manufacturer's service representative will interact with the design team, construction team, and most important, how they will respond to the client once the product or material has been installed. The product or material service program will be a very sensitive concern for the design professional and the client. Once this information has been systematically documented, it can then be analyzed by (a) the building design team, (b) the design professional in charge, (c) the specifier responsible for the project's execution, and (d) the client and the users. All persons involved in building design and construction should have the opportunity to analyze the documented information obtained from the manufacturer's response to determine fulfillment of identified performance criteria.

4. Contractor's Learning Experiences and Performance Records

The contractor should be asked to review material and product performance records so similar installations can be evaluated. Early involvement of the contractor can provide basic performance experiences that will allow the building design team to gain a more proper perspective for making the final building material selection and evaluation. This is especially true in the use of new products that have only been on the market for several months. Contractors can provide information about product installation, associated problems, and an overview of the performance after installation. A short period of surveillance can give valuable information as to how the product or material is responding to its environment. This information can be available from the contractor and should be documented in performance criteria records.

The contractor can also furnish information as to how the manufacturer supplied the product or material, and serviced it after installation. He can contribute performance information that should be investigated by both the client and the design professional before deciding on any material or product selections.

5. Client's Involvement in the Decision-Making Process

After documenting the manufacturer's and contractor's response to established performance criteria, the design professional and client should reevaluate all design decisions before making a final selection. Review the problem areas identified by the manufacturer and the contractor. Point out the risk areas and allow the client to take part in the final decision-making process. Once the design professional has defined potential problem areas, and taken into account all of the past experience and recorded research information, he will be in a good position in which to involve the client in the decision-making process. The design professional's guidance can help clarify the client's thinking and make it easier to arrive at a good decision. Documentation of all product decisions and potential risks will serve as a permanent record for the design professional and the client. If the design professional is called upon to prove that the proper precautions for making the final judgements about a building material or product were taken, this information will be valuable. It will show where the client was brought in to assist the final decisions as to whether or not to accept the associated risks pointed out in the selection process.

6. Structuring Specifications in Accordance With Performance Criteria

Once the design professional and client have made the final selection the manufacturer should assist in developing the appropriate specifications for the product in the contract documents. If the design professional develops his or her own specifications, the manufacturer should review the specifications and approve of them in writing. If the design professional does not prepare the specifications, they should be obtained from the manufacturer specifications that are in accordance with the performance criteria. The contractor should also be brought in when appropriate to review the specifications and the performance criteria. Any variations or possible problem areas should be studied before assigning the final contract. It is very crucial that the design professional obtain written approval for all decisions made in the development of material and product specifications. The specifications are an integral part of the contract documents that establish a material or product's development, installation and use.

7. Evaluation and Fulfillment of Performance Criteria

Performance criteria must be transferred to the design professional's or the manufacturer's specifier for evaluation and use in the final preparation of the product or material specifications. This is the point where all documented information and performance issues are taken into consideration by the person preparing the final specifications. Each statement made about the product's performance, installation, and use should be clearly stated and incorporated into established performance criteria. This provides the building design and construction team with an opportunity to understand the intent and goals to be fulfilled through the use of the product or material. The manufacturer's involvement during field installation should be identified. A field representative should be present to review the installation procedures that are established by the manufacturer and the contractor. Field installation procedures for the materials and products must be in accordance with the established performance criteria.

8. Recording Compliance with Specifications and Performance Criteria

Obtain from all building design team members, manufacturer's representatives, and contractors a compliance statement and checklist showing how the performance criteria and requirements set forth by the specifications were fulfilled. The manufacturer should identify the performance capabilities to prove that his product was developed to meet the performance criteria. These statements should be checked on the information matrix. The contractor should complete a written document stating how installation procedures were carried out in compliance with the specified requirements and in the presence of the manufacturer's representative. This information will indicate how each building team member fulfilled their responsibility in accordance with the contract. Any variations or changes should be documented in the appropriate section of performance criteria. Substitutions of building products or materials should be systematically reviewed according to the identified performance criteria. All decisions should be recorded with the appropriate performance criteria.

9. Comparing Actual Performance with Anticipated Performance

The information matrix containing a systematic approach to building material evaluation and selection will provide the framework for the final review of performance after installation. This review should be conducted during the final stages of installation, and continued while the material performs in its environment. With an identified list of performance criteria, the evaluator will be able to relate performance variables to issues originally established during early design stages. Changes in performance should be documented and correlated with the performance criteria. These will serve as historic data for future building design or for legal reference. This information will also allow the building technologist to identify the areas where the product or material was not able to perform in accordance with specifications. Accurate records will pinpoint what information was taken into account, what risks were identified, what performance criteria were fulfilled, where variations in performance are occurring, where potential problems may be developing, and who was responsible for making all of the decisions at each point in the building stage. The matrix of building performance criteria will provide the historic data to develop a better background of experience for each employee responsible for building design. Effective in-house education programs can be developed by simply using and studying the documented building material performance records from each project.

There are many legal implications for developing a systematic approach to evaluating and selecting building materials and products in the design professional's office. The development and perfection of a system will enable the design professional to serve his clients more effectively. By developing good internal records for future use, the design professional will also be able to provide his employees and clients with the following benefits:

- Documented performance records can be used to develop the employee's educational experience in the proper use of materials and products.
- The design professional will be in a better position to demonstrate his expertise and knowledge of building material performance to his clients.
- The design professional will be able to communicate and coordinate more effectively with his consultants and all members of the building team.
- Documented design decisions will provide the historic records for both the design professional and his client in the event of problems of building failures.
- An historic data file containing documented material and product performance records will enable the design professional to act objectively and competently in making all design decisions.
- Accurate files of former decisions and records of performance criteria fulfillment will enable the building design team to save time and money in responding to future design problems.
- Time and cost savings incurred by using the systematic approach can multiply as additional projects are developed under this system. The system's effectiveness will be discovered when the design professional is called upon to make an account of his decisions and professional acts.

A Systematic Approach to Achieve Building Material Performance

The initial selection of building materials and products is only a part of the responsibility to achieve total performance in a facility. The major part of the responsibility lies beyond the control of the design professional. To achieve accurate material performance, the design professional must describe the final performance and request the manufacturer and contractor carry out all specified procedures systematically. In many cases, the final performance tasks are not carried out systematically, or in a skilled manner. This usually results in building failure over which the design professional has little control because of the capabilities of other individuals outside of his contractual relationship.

Techniques are needed that allow the design professional to achieve a successful performance and develop control mechanisms beyond the original building material or product selection. Through the use of a systematic quality control program for identifying performance criteria and requirements, a certain control over other individuals responsible for the development and installation activities can be achieved. The manufacturer and the contractor should be brought in to act as team members in the very early stages of the decision making process. They have the opportunity to object or bring in new information in the building material and production selection process. The systematic listing of performance requirements and criteria will enable the design professional to establish a basis on which to communicate with all construction industry members responsible for providing and installing the materials and products.

Product and material development, production, and installation must all be accomplished with a complete understanding of the performance requirements that must be fulfilled. The quality control program must deal with two variables to achieve building material performance:

1. The material manufacturer.
2. The construction installer.

These two members of the building team have many employees responsible for developing and installing products and materials in accordance with established requirements. The question is: how does the design professional make them share the responsibilities for achieving successful material performance after the original selection process. By having the manufacturer and contractor a part of the building design and construction team, the design professional can develop a quality-control program based on fulfillment of design requirements and building material performance.

Product development criteria and installation requirements must be identified to show the manufacturer's and contractor's responsibilities for achieving building material performance. The criteria need to state tolerances, placement procedures, environmental conditions, labor requirements, personal experience, and other variables that must be dealt with in product development and field installation. These variables need to be presented and discussed by all team members early in the decision-making process. Problem areas should be reviewed with the client so he can understand the potential risk areas early in the decision making process.

An information matrix of performance requirements and criteria should be used to show the contractor and manufacturer standards they must comply with in development and installation. A checklist of performance criteria and noncompliance statements in developing an evaluation and selection record is essential. The information recorded in a performance matrix will be of great value to all members of the construction industry. The matrix not only forms the basis of communication, but can be used to specify responsibilities that must be fulfilled by each team member. The following steps and guidelines are crucial to develop a successful quality control program for achieving final building material and product performance:

1. Request all technical data from the manufacturer regarding a particular product or material and obtain the corresponding performance information.
2. Make the manufacturer and contractor a part of the design team. Have them prove that the material or product can be developed and installed in accordance with the performance requirements and criteria.
3. Make sure the manufacturer and contractor understand the specifications and special requirements and approve the installation.

4. Establish precontract conferences and document all decisions. Each individual must understand their responsibility.

5. Document the procedures used in installing the product or material and evaluate them against the manufacturer's installation requirements.

6. Have the subcontractors perform on-site tests and sign statements that the application was carried out in accordance with the manufacturer's directions.

7. Have the general contractor verify all tests and sign the approved shop drawings developed by the manufacturer.

8. Have the manufacturer, general contractor, and the subcontractors file compliance statements indicating that they complied with all performance requirements and criteria and fulfilled the product development and field installation procedures.

9. The design professional should prepare a final report that contains all of the written statements submitted by the manufacturers, contractors, and all consultants stating that they fulfilled the performance requirements and criteria. This will provide the framework for developing an effective building material performance record after construction. All variations in performance can be documented and historic data files can be established. **These records will serve three purposes: (a) A future reference source for design professionals conducting material and product evaluation and selection programs. (b) A record for later reference in the event that a failure occurs. (c) As valuable material and information source for training new employees in building material evaluation and selection.**

Glossary

ENVIRONMENTAL FACTORS

The interaction of natural and synthetic forces that contribute toward making a change in an object or facility.

FACTOR ANALYSIS

Is a mathematical procedure that resolves a set of descriptive variables into a smaller number of categories, components, or factors. It could be a useful tool in determining all parameters of a problem and setting up a scientific hypotheses in design.

MATRIX ANALYSIS

A form of mathematics that provides a systematic method for the manipulation and solution of systems of equations. The matrix is a rectangular array of numbers, called elements, arranged in rows and columns.

OPERATIONS RESEARCH

Is the use of a scientific method in providing executive departments with a quantitive basis for decisions regarding the operations under their control.

PERFORMANCE CRITERIA

Identified standards, that indicate a level of performance essential to fulfill human needs, on which a judgement, evaluation, and decision can be based. They collectively provide a basis for determining whether a selection or solution fulfills the identified requirements.

PERFORMANCE REQUIREMENTS

Technical statements developed from identified user needs and objectives

131

that indicate an expected level of performance in order to fulfill a given function.

PERFORMANCE VARIABLES

Observed changes in the material or product that differs from its anticipated and projected performance. Field observation will identify these changes in performance over a given period of time.

QUALITY CONTROL

Measures of control in production and development that insures a product or the facility fulfills the performance requirements and meets the needs and expectations of the client.

SYSTEM ANALYSIS

Is a procedure for studying the structure of a complex interacting or interdependent group of items forming a unified whole.

SYSTEMATIC APPROACH

A step-by-step plan in gathering and organizing interacting or interdependent items of information in a decision making process.

USER NEEDS

Identifiable human needs (physiological, sociological, and psychological) resulting from the performance of daily living or working activities.

References

Anderson, Clyde E. Address to the Construction Contracts and Specifications Institute. University of Wisconsin, November 7, 1974.

Fletcher, Sir Banister. *A History of Architecture on the Comparative Method,* 16th edition. New York: Charles Scribner's Sons, 1956.

Maslow, A. H. *The Farther Reaches of Human Nature.* New York: Viking Press, 1971.

Appendix

BUILDING, HOUSING, AND ALLIED RESEARCH CENTERS THROUGHOUT THE WORLD

The world wide need for building research, and for the exchange of information, continues to increase. With the development of links between research organizations in different countries, and the expansion of international construction activity, it has become of even greater value to know the addresses of leading building research centers in other countries. The lists given in this Note are offered as some help in this regard, although they are not claimed to be comprehensive. In some countries all building research is carried out in a single government research station, and the address of this station has been given whenever possible. In other countries research is shared between government stations, the universities, and private industry. In such cases it has been inpracticable to list every laboratory, and so an attempt has been made to identify the prime organization, from which further information might be obtained about the activities of other institutes. Furthermore although in many cases fire research, timber research and geotechnics research are also carried out by the central building research institute, yet in other cases these subjects are studied at separate laboratories. It is therefore advisable to consider this note only as an initial guide, rather than as a comprehensive reference. The organiza-

Reprinted from Overseas Building Note No. 163 (revised November 1978), by permission of the Building Research Establishment.

tions listed herein may be the major sources of research information for the countries concerned, but before making substantial enquiries of any institute it would be sensible to obtain details of its services, charges and fields of interest.

INTERNATIONAL ORGANIZATIONS

United Nations Industrial Development
Organization (UNIDO)
PO Box 707
A 1011 VIENNA, AUSTRIA

Educational Facilities Section
Division of Educational Policy and
Planning (UNESCO)
7 Place de Fontenoy
75700 PARIS, FRANCE

International Union of Testing and
Research Laboratories for Materials
and Structures (RILEM)
12 Rue Brancion
75737 PARIS CEDEX 15, FRANCE

International Council for Building
Research Studies and Documentation
(CIB)
Weena 704
Post Box 20704
3001 JA ROTTERDAM,
NETHERLANDS

International Organization for
Standardization (ISO)
1 Rue de Varembé
1211 GENEVA, SWITZERLAND

Center for Housing, Building, and
Planning
1 UN Plaza, 15th Floor
United Nations
NEW YORK 10017, USA

United Nations Office of Technical Co-
operation (OTC)
United Nations
NEW YORK 10017, USA

The Assistant Director for Technical
Services
Office of Housing
United States Agency for International
Development
Department of State
WASHINGTON DC 20523, USA

Environmental Liaison Center (UNEP)
PO Box 72461
NAIROBI, KENYA

AFRICA

Regional organizations

UNESCO Regional Office for
Education in Africa
PO Box 3311
DAKAR, SENEGAL

UN Economic Commission for Africa
(ECA)
Housing, Building and Physical
Planning Section
PO Box 3001
ADDIS ABABA, ETHIOPIA

Algeria

National Laboratory of Public Works
and Building (LNTPB)
Route des 4 Canons
ALGER

Algerian Building Research Institute
Oued Smar
El Harrach, ALGER

Angola

Laboratory of Engineering of Angola
Caixa Postal 6500
LUANDA

Benin

Regional Office (CEBTP)
BP 1270
COTONOU

Botswana

The Chief Architect
Ministry of Works and
  Communications
PO Box 0025
GABORONE

Ministry of Local Government and
  Lands
Private Bag 006
GABORONE

Cameroon

Regional Office (CEBTP)
BP 2004
YAOUNDE

Central African Empire

Regional Office (CEBTP)
BP 846
BANGUI

Congo Republic

National Laboratory for Research and
  Public Works
BP 752
BRAZZAVILLE

Egypt

General Organisation for Housing,
  Building and Planning Research
PO Box 1770
El-Tahreer Street
Dokky, CAIRO

Ethiopia

Ethiopian Standards Institute
Department of Commerce and Industry
PO Box 2310
ADDIS ABABA

Housing Development and Research
  Department
Ministry of Housing and Urban
  Development
PO Box 3386
ADDIS ABABA

Regional Housing Officer
US AID/Ethiopia
PO Box 1014
ADDIS ABABA

Gabon

Regional Office (CEBTP)
BP 766
LIBREVILLE

Ghana

Council for Scientific and Industrial
  Research
PO Box M32
ACCRA

CSIR Building and Road Research
  Institute
University Post Box 40, UST
KUMASI

Faculty of Architecture
University of Science and Technology
KUMASI

CSIR Forest Products Research
  Institute
University Post Box 63, UST
KUMASI

Ivory Coast

Research Centre for Architecture and
  Town Planning (CRAU)
Université d'Abidjan
BP 8892
ABIDJAN

Department of Public Works
Laboratory of Building and Public
  Works
BP 4003
ABIDJAN

Kenya

Ministry of Works
PO Box 11873
NAIROBI

University of Nairobi
Department of Civil Engineering
PO Box 30197
NAIROBI
(Includes wood Research)

Housing Research and Development
  Unit
Department of Architecture
University of Nairobi
PO Box 30197
NAIROBI

Liberia

Soils/Materials Testing and Research
  Division
Bureau of Technical Services
Ministry of Public Works
MONROVIA

The National Housing Authority
UN Drive—Water Street
MONROVIA

Libya

The Technical Planning Authority
PO Box 600
TRIPOLI

The Industrial Research Centre
Building Materials Unit
PO Box 3633
TRIPOLI

Madagascar

Regional Office (CEBTP)
BP 1151
ANTANANARIVO

Malawi

Malawi Housing Corporation
PO Box 414
BLANTYRE

Mauritania

Regional Office (CEBTP)
BP 602
NAUAKCHOTT

Mauritius

Regional Office (CEBTP)
PHOENIX

Mozambique

Laboratorio de Enghenaria de
  Moçambique
Ave de Moçambique
CP 1918
CON PHUMO

Morocco

Public Works Department Testing and
  Research Laboratory
25 rue d'Azilal
BP 667
CASABLANCA

Nigeria

Forestry Research Institute of Nigeria
PMB 5054
IBADAN

Federal Ministry of Works
Civil Engineering Services Division
PMB 12635
15 Awolowo Road
SW Ikoyi
LAGOS

Federal Housing Authority
Department of Planning and Research
Badagry Road
PMB 3200
Suru-lere
LAGOS

Senegal

African Institute for Economic
  Development and Planning
BP 3186
DAKAR

Regional Office (CEBTP)
BP 189
DAKAR

Somali Democratic Republic

National Housing Agency
MOGADISHU

South Africa

National Building Research Institute
PO Box 395
PRETORIA 0001

140   Appendix

The South African Forestry Research
   Institute
PO Box 727
PRETORIA 0001

Sudan

Building and Road Research Institute
University of Khartoum
PO Box 35
KHARTOUM

Tanzania

Building Research Unit
PO Box 1964
DAR ES SALAAM

Tanzania National Scientific Research
   Council
PO Box 4302
DAR ES SALAAM

University of Dar es Salaam
Faculty of Engineering
PO Box 35131
DAR ES SALAAM

Togo Republic

Centre for Building and Housing
BP 911
LOMÉ

Uganda

Ministry of Agriculture and Forestry
Forest Products Office
PO Box 1752
KAMPALA

Building Research Unit
Central Materials Laboratory
Ministry of Housing and Public
   Buildings
PO Box 7188
KAMPALA

Upper Volta

Regional Office (CEBTP)
BP 133
OUAGADOUGOU

Zaire Republic

Department of Public Works
Civil Building Directorate
BP 27A
KINSHASA-GOMBE

Regional Office (CEBTP)
BP 1403
KINSHASA

Zambia

National Housing Authority
PO Box RW 74
Ridgeway
LUSAKA

National Council for Scientific
   Research
PO Box CH 158
Chelston
LUSAKA

AMERICA

Regional organizations

Office of Research and Technology
Department of Housing and Urban
Development
Organization of American States
WASHINGTON DC 20401, USA

Servico Interamericano de Informacion
Sobre Desarollo Urbano
(Sindu-Nal)
Apartado Aéreo 6209
BOGOTA, COLOMBIA

Economic Commission for Latin
America (ECLA)
SANTIAGO, CHILE

Regional Forestry Officer
FAO Regional Office
Casilla 10095
SANTIAGO, CHILE

Regional School Building Centre for
Latin America (CONESCAL)
Apartado Postal 41–518
MEXICO 10, DF

Argentina

Department of Research and
Technology of the State Secretariat
for Housing
Defensa 120–3º Piso
BUENOS AIRES

Research and Information Centre for
Construction and Housing of the
National Institute of Industrial
Technology
Bouwcentrum Argentina
Casilla de Correo 157
Suc S Martin
BUENOS AIRES

Laboratory for Materials Testing and
Technological Research (LEMIT)
Calle 52–121 y 122
La Plata, BUENOS AIRES

Bolivia

National Scientific and Technological
Documentation Centre
Casilla Correo No 3283
LA PAZ

Materials Testing Institute
Casilla Correo No 8653
LA PAZ

Architecture and Urbanism Institute
Casilla Correo No 8653
LA PAZ

Brazil

National Housing Research Centre
(CENPHA)
Rua Marques de sao Vincente 225
Gavea, ZC–20–GB
RIO DE JANEIRO

Brazilian Building Centre
Bouwcentrum
Praca Roosevelt 183
Esquina Gravatai
C Postal 9530
SAO PAULO

142   Appendix

Institute of Technology
Biblioteca Central
Cidade Universitaria
05508 SAO PAULO

Centre of Social Studies of Housing and
Town Planning (NEURB)
Rua Marques de Sao Vicente 209
RIO DE JANEIRO

Canada

National Research Council
Division of Building Research
Montreal Road
OTTAWA KIA OR6

Department of the Environment
Eastern Forest Products Laboratory
Montreal Road
OTTAWA K1G 3Z5

Department of the Environment
Western Forest Products Laboratory
6620 Northwest Marine Drive
VANCOUVER V6T 1X2

Chile

Centre for Housing and Construction
Universidad de Chile
Casilla 5373
SANTIAGO

Forest Products Laboratory
School of Engineering
Universidad de Concepción
Casilla 53–C
CONCEPCIÓN

Columbia

Institute of Construction
Universidad del Valle
Apartado Nacional no 439
CALI

National Centre for Construction
   Studies (CENAC)
Ciudad Universitaria
Cll 45–cra 30
Edificio CINVA
AA 34219
BOGOTA

Forestry and Timber Research Institute
Universidad Distrital
Francisco José de Caldas
Apartado Aéreo 8668
BOGOTA

Institute of Technology
Apartado Aéreo 7031
BOGOTA

Costa Rica

National Institute of Housing and
   Planning
PO Box 2534
SAN JOSÉ

CATIE Forest Products Laboratory
University of Costa Rica
PO Box 36
SAN JOSÉ

Cuba

Centre for Building Research (CIEC)
Apartado 6180
HAVANA

Ministry of Construction
Plaza de la Revolucion
Zona Postal 6
HAVANA

El Salvador

Ministry of Public Works
41 Avenida Norte 221
SAN SALVADOR

The National University
SAN SALVADOR

Central-American Technical Institute
Civil Engineering and Building
  Department
Apartado No 1783
SANTA TECLA

French Guiana

Regional Office (CEBTP)
BP 297
CAYENNE

Guatemala

Central American Research Institute
  for Industry (ICAITI)
Apartado Postal 1552
Avenida La Reforma 4–47
Zona 12
GUATEMALA

Building Information Center
School for Engineering
Ciudad Universitaria
Zona 12
GUATEMALA

Republic of Haiti

Regional Office (CEBTP)
Rue du Magasin de L'Etat
PORT AU PRINCE

Honduras

Ministry of Communications, Public
  Works and Transportation
Barrio La Bolsa
COMAYAGUELA, DC

Jamaica

Ministry of Housing
PO Box 397
KINGSTON 10

Martinique

Regional Office (CEBTP)
Carrefour Redoute Entraide
BP 991
FORT DE FRANCE

Mexico

National Institute for Workers Housing
  (INFONAVIT)
Apartado Postal 41–518
MEXICO DF

Information and Documentation Centre
National Council for Science &
  Technology
Insurgentes Sur 1677
MEXICO 20 DF

Panama

Materials Testing Laboratory
Centro Experimental de Ingenieria
Instituto Politecnico
Estafeta Universitaria
PANAMA

Paraguay

National Institute of Technology and
Standards (INTN)
Casilla de Correo 967
ASUNCIÓN

Peru

Ministry of Housing and Construction
Experimental Housing Project
(PREVI)
Panamericana Norte 16900
Artopista Ancón
LIMA

Ministry of Agriculture and Food
Cahuide No 805
LIMA 11
(Includes forestry and fire research)

Department of Structural Engineering
Universidad Nacional de Ingenieria
Casilla 1301
LIMA

Itintec Institute of Technology
Jr Morelli 2 da Cdra
Esq Avda las Artes
San Borja
LIMA 34

Puerto Rico

Urban Renewal and Housing
  Administration
Box 20591
RIO PIEDRAS

Southern Forest Experimental Station
United States Department of
  Agriculture
Forest Service
Box AQ
RIO PIEDRAS

Trinidad

Caribbean Industrial Research Institute
  (CARIRI)
Tunapuna Post Office
TRINIDAD

United States

Building Research Advisory Board
National Research Council
2101 Constitution Avenue
WASHINGTON, DC 20418

National Bureau of Standards
Center for Building Technology
WASHINGTON, DC 20234

American Society for Testing Materials
  (ASTM)
1916 Race Street
PHILADELPHIA, PA 19103

US Department of Agriculture
Forest Service
Forest Products Laboratory
PO Box 5130
MADISON, WISCONSIN 53705

National Institute of Building Sciences
1730 Pennsylvania Avenue, NW
WASHINGTON, DC 20006

ASIA

Regional Organizations

Uruguay

Materials Testing Institute
Julio M Sosa 2181
MONTEVIDEO

Institute of Civil Engineering
J Herrera y Reisig 565
MONTEVIDEO

Venezuela

National Forest Products Laboratory
Apartado 220
MERIDA

Institute of Experimental Building
   Development (IDEC)
Central University of Caracas
Faculty of Architecture and Town
   Planning
Apartado de Correos 59169
CARACAS 104

Venezuelan National Council for
   Scientific and Technical Research
   (CONICIT)
Final Avenue Principal Los Cortyos de
   Lourdes
Edifico Maploca
Apartado Postal: 70.617
Los Ruices
CARACAS

Economic Commission for Western Asia
   (ECWA)
PO Box 4656
BEIRUT, LEBANON

Economic and Social Commission for
   Asia and the Pacific (ESCAP)
Division of Industry and Housing
Housing and Building Planning Section
United Nations Building
Rajdamnern Avenue
BANGKOK, THAILAND

UNESCO Regional Office for
   Education in Asia
Darakarn Building
920 Sukhumvit Road
CPO Box 1425
BANGKOK, THAILAND

Asian Institute of Technology (AIT)
PO Box 2754
Rangsit
BANGKOK, THAILAND

United National Regional Housing
   Centre for ESCAP
National Buildings Organisation
Nirman Bhawan
Maulana Azad Road
NEW DELHI—110011, INDIA

UN Regional Housing Centre
PO Box 15
84 Jalan Tamansari
BANDUNG, INDONESIA

Bangladesh

Housing and Building Research
Institute
Ministry of Public Works and Urban
Development
Mirpur
DACCA

Bangladesh University of Engineering
and Technology (BUET)
DACCA 2

Bahrain

Department of Building and Civil
Engineering
Gulf Technical College
ISA TOWN

Burma

National Construction Corporation
Building Research Laboratory
Kamakyi Road
Thuwamma
RANGOON

China

Technical Information Institute
Academy of Building Research
19 Che Kung Chuang Street
PO Box 7520
PEKING

Hong Kong

Faculty of Engineering
University of Hong Kong
Pokfulam Road

School of Architecture
University of Hong Kong
Pokfulam Road

India

Ministry of Works and Housing
Central Building Research Institute
(CBRI)
ROORKEE (UP)

Housing and Urban Development
Corporation
Jam Nagar House
NEW DELHI—12

Public Works Department Research
Institute
LUCKNOW (UP)

Structural Engineering Research
(Regional) Centre
Council of Scientific and Industrial
Research
CSIR Campus
Adyar
MADRAS—600 020

National Buildings Organisation
Ministry of Works and Housing
5th Floor, Nirman Bhawan, G Wing
Maulana Azad Road
NEW DELHI 110011

Public Works Department
Soil Mechanics and Research Division
Chepauk
MADRAS 600 005

Forest Research Institute and College
PO Newforest
DEHRADUN

Indonesia

Directorate of Building Research
PO Box 15
84 Jalan Tamansari
BANDUNG

Building Information Centre
20 Jalan Pattimura
Kebayoran Baru
JAKARTA SELATAN

Centre for Urban and Environmental
  Research
Jakarta Municipal Building
8–9 Jalan Merdeka Selatan
Block G, Lantai 22
JAKARTA PUSAT

Iran

Ministry of Housing and Urban
  Development
Building and Housing Research Center
PO Box 15–1114
TEHRAN

Iraq

Building Research Centre
Scientific Research Foundation
PO Box 127
Jadiriyah
BAGHDAD

National Centre for Testing
  Laboratories
Ministry of Housing and Construction
BAGHDAD

Israel

Building Research Station—
  TECHNION
Israel Institute of Technology
Technion City
HAIFA

Building and Techniques Research
  Institute
The Engineers' Institute
200 Dizengoff Road
PO Box 3082
TEL-AVIV

Building Centre of Israel
PO Box 7102
TEL-AVIV

Industrial Research Administration
Israel Fiber Institute
5 Emek Refaim Street
PO Box 8001
JERUSALEM
(Includes wood preservation)

Japan

Building Research Institute
Ministry of Construction
No 1 Tatehara, Oh-ho-machi
Tsukuba—Gun
IBARAKI—PREF

The Building Centre of Japan
14–16 Harumi 1—Chome
Chuo-Kuo
TOKYO

Japan International Co-operation
  Agency (JICA)
PO Box 216 Mitsui Bldg
2–1 Nishi-Shinjuku, Shinjuku-Ku
TOKYO

Forestry and Forest Products Research
   Institute
PO Box 2
Ushiki
IBARAKI, 300–12

Jordan

Building Materials Research Centre
Royal Scientific Society
PO Box 6945
AMMAN

Korea

National Construction Research
   Institute
Ministry of Construction
IPO 2159
SEOUL

Korea Scientific and Technical
   Information Centre
IPO Box 1229
SEOUL

Kuwait

Kuwait Institute for Scientific Research
PO Box 12009
KUWAIT

Research Station
Ministry of Public Works
PO Box 8
KUWAIT

Lebanon

National Council of Scientific Research
Sports City Boulevard
BEIRUT

Ministry of Public Works and
   Transport
Materials and Soil Laboratory
Dekwany
BEIRUT

Faculty of Engineering and
   Architecture
American University of Beirut
BEIRUT

Malaysia

Mara Institute of Technology
Shah Alam
SELANGOR
(Architecture, Planning etc.)

Materials Testing Laboratory
Public Works Dept
Kota Kinbalu
SABAH

Forest Research Institute
Kepong
SALÀNGOR

University of Malaya
Pantai Valley
KUALA LUMPUR 22–11
(Includes materials exposure site)

Nepal

Department of Housing, Building and
   Physical Planning
Babar Mahal
KATHMANDU

Applied Science and Technology
   Research Centre
Tribhuvan University
Kirtipur
KATHMANDU

Oman

Ministry of Social Affairs and Labour
Vocational training centre
PO Box 3123
RUWI

Pakistan

Punjab Building Research Station
Council for Works and Housing
   Research
PO Box No 1230
LAHORE

Building Research Station
Council for Works and Housing
   Research
F/40 SITE, Hub River Road
KARACHI 28

Philippines

National Institute of Science and
   Technology
POB 774
MANILA

National Housing Authority
Elliptical Road
Diliman
QUEZON CITY

Forest Products Research and
   Industries Development Commission
College
LAGUNA 3720

Saudi Arabia

Research Center
College of Engineering
University of Riyad
PO Box 800
RIYAD

Singapore

University of Singapore
Faculty of Architecture and Building
Department of Building Science
Kent Ridge Campus
off Clementi Road
Kent Ridge
SINGAPORE 5

Institute of Standards and Industrial
   Research
179 River Valley Road
SINGAPORE 6

Singapore Housing and Development
   Board
Maxwell Road
SINGAPORE

Sri Lanka

Building Research Institute
State Engineering Corporation of Sri
   Lanka
99/1 Jawatte Road
COLOMBO 5

Ceylon Institute of Scientific and
   Industrial Research
PO Box 787
COLOMBO 7

Syria

UN Centre for Housing and
  Construction
PO Box 2317
DAMASCUS

Taiwan

Chinese Institute of Civil and
  Hydraulic Engineering
4th Floor, 1 Jen Ai Road, Sec 2
PO Box 499
TAIPEI

Forest Research Institute
Botanical Gardens
Nan Hai Road
TAIPEI

Thailand

National Housing Authority
Research and Planning Department
Klongchan, Bangkapi
BANGKOK 24

Wood Protection Section
Forest Products Research Division
Royal Forest Department
BANGKOK 9

Applied Scientific Research
  Corporation of Thailand (ASRCT)
Bangkhen
BANGKOK 9

Turkey

Building Research Institute
Scientific and Technical Research
  Council of Turkey
Ataturk Bulvari 243
Kavaklidere
ANKARA

Building Research Centre
Yapi Arastirma Kurumu
Teknik Université
ISTANBUL

University of Istanbul
Faculty of Forestry
Department of Wood Technology
Büyükdere
ISTANBUL

United Arab Emirates

Department of Research and Studies
Ministry of Public Works and Housing
PO Box 1828
DUBAI

USSR

Research Department
Gosstroi USSR
Prospekt Marksa 43
MOSCOW K–25

Scientific Research Institute
CNIISK (Structural Engineering)
2 Institutskaja 6
MOSCOW

AUSTRALASIA

Australia

Commonwealth Scientific and
  Industrial Research Organisation
Division of Building Research
PO Box 56
MELBOURNE
VICTORIA 3190

Experimental Building Station
Department of Construction
PO Box 30
CHATSWOOD 2067

French Polynesia

Regional Office (CEBTP)
BP 404
PAPEETE

New Caledonia

Regional Office (CEBTP)
Route de Doniambo
BP 821
NOUMEA

New Zealand

Building Research Association of New
  Zealand
42 Vivian Street
PO Box 9375
WELLINGTON

Forest Research Institute
Private Bag
ROTORUA

Timber Research and Development
  Association (TRADA)
PO Box 308
WELLINGTON

Papua New Guinea

Papua New Guinea University of
  Technology
PO Box 793
LAE

Research and Development Officer
National Housing Commission
PO Box 1550
BOROKO

Department of Forests
Forest Products Research Centre
PO Box 1358
BOROKO

EUROPE

Regional Organizations

United Nations Economic Commission
  for Europe (ECE)
Palais des Nations
CH—1211 GENEVA 10,
SWITZERLAND

Austria

Austrian Institute for Building
  Research
Dr Karl Luegar-Ring 10
A—1010, VIENNA 1

152   Appendix

Austrian Association for Housing
  Research
Löwengasse 47
Mezzanin
Fach 164
A–1031 VIENNA III

Austrian Institute for Wood Research
Franz-grille-strasse 7
Arsenal
A 1030 VIENNA

Institute for Construction and
  Architecture
Slovak Academy of Sciences
PO Box 1191 Dubravska cesta
885 46 BRATISLAVA

State Forest Products Research
  Institute
5 Lamacska cesta
BRATISLAVA

Belgium

Scientific and Technical Building
  Centre (CSTC)
Rue du Lombard 41
1000 BRUSSELS

National Fire Protection Association
Rue de l'Autonomie 4
1070 BRUSSELS

Bulgaria

Building Research Institute (NISI)
Boulevard Petko Napetov 36
SOFIA

Institute for Forest and Wood
  Technology
Department of Wood Technology
Gelu Voivoda 10–VLTI
SOFIA–56

Czechoslovakia

Research Institute for Building and
  Architecture (VUVA)
Letenska 3, Mala Strana
PRAGUE 1

Denmark

Danish Building Research Institute
SBI Post Box 119
DK–2970 HORSHOLM

The Building Centre
Byggecentrum
Glydenlovesgade 19
DK–1600 COPENHAGEN V

The Nordic Committee on Building
  Regulations Secretariat
Boligministeriet
Slotsholmgade 12
DK–1216 COPENHAGEN K

Department of Wood Technology
Teknologisk Institute
Gregersensvej
DK–2630 TASTRUP

Eire

National Institute for Physical Planning
  and Construction Research
St Martin's House
Waterloo Road
DUBLIN 4

Institute for Industrial Research and
Standards
Industrial Research Centre
Ballymun Road
DUBLIN 9

The Building Centre
4 Northbrook Road
DUBLIN 6

Federal Republic of Germany

Building Research Institute
An der Markuskirche 1
3000 HANOVER 1

Federal Materials Testing
Establishment
BAM, Abt 2, Bauwesen
Unter den Eichen 87
1000—BERLIN—45

Tropical Building Institute
Waldschmidstrasse 6A
813 STARNBERG

Federal Research Centre for Forestry
and Forest Products
Leuschnerstrasse 91
D—2050 HAMBURG 80

Research Institute for Fire Fighting
Techniques
University of Karlsruhe
Hertzstrasse 16
PO Box 6380
D—7500 KARLSRUHE 21

IRB Informations verbundzentrum
RAUM and BAU der
Fraunhofergesellschaft
Silberbergstrasse 119A
7000 STUTTGART 1

Finland

Technical Research Centre of Finland
Vuorimiehentie 5
02150 ESPOO 15

Building Information Institute
Lonnrotinkatu 20B
00120 HELSINKI 12

Technical Research Centre of Finland
Fire Technology Laboratory
Vuorimiehentie 4
02150 ESPOO 15

Technical Research Centre of Finland
Timber Laboratory
Puumiehenkuya 2A
02150 ESPOO 15

France

Scientific and Technical Building
Centre (CSTB)
4 Avenue du Recteur-Poincaré
75782 PARIS CÉDEX 16

Experimental Centre for Study and
Research on Building and Public
Works (CEBTP)
12 Rue Brancion
75015 PARIS CÉDEX 15

(Has 13 laboratories in the following
countries:
**Benin, New Caledonia, Cameroon,
Central African Empire, French
Guiana, Gabon, Haiti, Madagascar,
Martinique, Mauritania, Mauritius,
French Polynesia, Upper Volta.** See
individual countries for addresses.)

Technical Advisory Centre for Building
and Public Works (CATED)
c/o UTI
9 Rue de la Pérouse
75784–PARIS CÉDEX 16

Secretariat of Town Planning and
Housing Missions
Secrétariat des Missions d'Urbanisme et
d'Habitat (SMUH)
11 rue Chardin
75016 PARIS

Technical Centre for Tropical Forestry
45 bis, Avenue de la Belle-Gabrielle
F–94130 NOGENT-SUR-MARNE

Station de Recherche de Champs-sur-
Marne
84 Avenue Jean Jaures
77420 CHAMPS-SUR-MARNE
(deals with fire research)

German Democratic Republic

Technical University of Dresden
(Building Engineering Section)
Sektion Bauingenieurwesen
Mommsenstrasse 13
8027 DRESDEN

Building Academy of the German
Democratic Republic
Scharrenstrasse 2/3
102 BERLIN

Academy of Sciences of the GDR
Central Earth Physics Institute
Burgweg 11
69 JENA

Greece

Public Works Research Center
Ministry of Public Works (KEDE)
166 Piraeus Street
ATHENS 310

Hungary

Hungarian Institute for Building
Science (ETI)
David Ferenc utca 6
Postafiok 71
1113 BUDAPEST

Building Information Centre
Hársfa utca 21
Postafiok 83
1400 BUDAPEST VII

Institute of Design Development and
System Design
Asbóth utca 9–11
Postafiok 369
1370 BUDAPEST VII

Iceland

The Building Research Institute
Rannsoknastofnun
Byggingaridnadarins
Keldnaholt
REYKJAVIK

Italy

Italian Association for the Promotion of
Building Research and Studies
(AIRE)
Via Beato Angelico 3
20133 MILAN

Central Institute for Building
   Technology (ICITE)
National Research Council
Via Lombardia 49
San Giuliano Milanese
20098 MILAN

Institute of Wood
National Research Council
Villa Favorita
Piazza T A Edison 11
50133 FLORENCE

Centre for Fire Prevention Studies
Piazza Scilla 2
00178 ROME–CAPANELLE

Luxemburg

Testing Materials Laboratory
Administration des Ponts et Chaussées
7–11 Rue Albert 1er
LUXEMBURG

Society for Study of Technical
   Construction
2 rue des Sapins
Senningerberg
LUXEMBURG

National Society for Low-cost dwellings
   (SNHBM)
108 Avenue du 10 Septembre
LUXEMBURG

Netherlands

Information Department
Netherlands Organisation for Applied
   Scientific Research (TNO)
PO Box 297
2501 BD THE HAGUE

Information Centre for School Building
PO Box 299
3000 AG ROTTERDAM

Head of International Relations
   Division
Ministry of Housing and Physical
   Planning
85 Von Alkemadelaan
THE HAGUE

The Building Centre
Bouwcentrum
700 Weena, PO Box 299
ROTTERDAM

Norway

Norwegian Building Research Institute
Forskningsveien 3B
Postboks 322, Blindern
OSLO 3

The Norwegian Building Centre
Haakon VII S gate 2
Postboks 1575, Vika
OSLO 1

Norwegian Institute of Wood
   Technology
Forskningsveien 3B
Postboks 331, Blindern
OSLO 3

Norwegian Fire Research Laboratory
7034 TRONDHEIM–NTH

Poland

Building Research Institute
ul. Filtrowa l, Skr. Poczt 998
00–950 WARSAW

Centre for Building Information
ul. Senatorska
00–950 WARSAW

Institute of Wood Preservation
(SGGW)
ul. Rakowiecka 26/30
WARSAW

Portugal

Ministry of Housing and Public Works
Praça do Comércio
LISBON 1

Institute for the Construction Industry
Rua Castilho, 50
LISBON 1

Romania

Building Research Institute (INCERC)
Ses Pantelimon Nr 266–Sectorul 3
BUCHAREST

Institute for Research and Development
in Town Planning, Housing and
Public Works (ISLGC)
Str Snagov 53–55
BUCHAREST 13

Bucharest University
Department of Geotechnics and
Foundations
B-Dul Lacul Tei 124
BUCHAREST

Institute for Research and Development
for Industry
Lemnulii
Soseaua Pipera 46 sector 2
BUCHAREST
(Includes timber research)

Brasov University
Woodworking Industry Faculty
Colina Universitatii
BRASOV

Spain

Eduardo Torroja Institute for Building
and Cement Research
Costillares–Chamartin
MADRID–33

Ministry of Public Works and Town
Planning
Plaza de San Juan de la Crux, 2
MADRID–3

Construction Information Centre (CIC)
Lauria 117
BARCELONA–9

Sweden

The National Swedish Institute for
Building Research (SIB)
Box 785
S–801 29 GÄVLE

The Swedish International
Development Authority (SIDA)
Birger Jarlsgatan 61
S–105 25 STOCKHOLM
(Includes assistance with low-cost
housing abroad)

The Swedish Forest Products Research
Laboratory
PO Box 5604
S–114 86 STOCKHOLM

Swedish Building Centre (SB)
Master Samuelsgatan 38
PO Box 1403
S–111 84 STOCKHOLM

Swedish National Testing Institute
Box 857
S–501 15 BORAS

Switzerland

Swiss Federal Department of Housing
Weltpoststrasse 4
Postfach 38
3000 BERNE 15

Swiss Federal Laboratories for
  Materials Testing and Research
Institute for Industry, Building and
  Trade (EMPA)
Uberlandstrasse 129
8600 DÜBENDORF

United Kingdom

Building Research Establishment
Building Research Station
Garston
WATFORD WD2 7JR

Building Research Establishment
Fire Research Station
BOREHAMWOOD WD6 2BL

Building Research Establishment
Princes Risborough Laboratory
Princes Risborough
AYLESBURY HP17 9PX

The Building Centre
26 Store Street
LONDON WC1E 7BT

Construction Industry Research and
  Information Association (CIRIA)
6 Storeys Gate
LONDON SW1P 3AU

The Timber Research and
  Development Association (TRADA)
Hughenden Valley
HIGH WYCOMBE

Intermediate Technology Development
  Group Ltd
9 King Street
LONDON WC2E 8HN

Yugoslavia

Yugoslav Building Centre
Bulevar Revolucije 84
11000 BELGRADE

Institute for Testing and Research in
  Materials and Structures
Dimiceva 12
61000 LJUBLJANA

Institute for Civil Engineering and
  Building Construction
Janka Rakuse 1
41000 ZAGREB

Faculty of Forestry
Institute for Woodworking
Wood Protection Section
Kreza Viseslava 1
11030 BELGRADE

Index

ANSI standards, 4
ASTM standards, 4, 43
ASTM test methods, 27, 44
"Attributes," 16, 18, 22

Building codes, 80
Building construction, costs, 54
  legal problems, 58
  number of people involved in, 57
  performance approach, 6
  quality control, 55
  responsibilities, 58
Building design, legal problems, 58
  number of people involved in, 57
  responsibility, 58
Building design process, systematic
  approach, 117
Building design team, application of
  systematic approach, 107
Building materials, analyzation, 54
  insurance ratings, 110
  research programs, 71, 72
  substitutions, 126
  systems approach to selection of,
  175
Building materials evaluation, 100,
  108, 123
  performance criteria, 120
  program, 122
  systematic approach, legal implications, 126
Building Materials performance, 127,
  129
  criteria, 116
  records, 130
  systematic approach, 127, 128
Building materials selection, 100,
  108, 123

performance criteria, 120
  systematic approach, legal implications, 126
Building materials selection process,
  systematic approach, 107, 108
Building performance criteria,
  matrix, 126
  systematic approach, 118
Building performance evaluation,
  115, 116
Building product evaluation, systematic approach, legal implications,
  126
Building product performance, 129
Building products, performance
  criteria, 116
  substitution, 126
Building product selection, systematic approach, legal implications,
  126
Building Research Establishment, 23
"Building technology," 59

Client input, 116, 117
Client responsibility, 116, 117
Compliance, with identified per-
  formance criteria, 122, 123
  statements of, 122
Compliance statement, performance
  criteria, 125, 126
  performance requirement, 125, 126
Computerized Evaluation Matrix, 94
Computer program, benefits, 95
Computer selection, 64
COMSPEC Services, 68
Construction information systems,
  64, 68, 69, 103
Construction installer, 128-130

Construction language, universally
accepted, 103
Construction manager, 45
Construction Specifications Insti-
tute's Programs Spec-Data I and
II, 68
Contract documents, 90, 114, 124
Contractor, 45, 114, 123
liabilities, 61, 62
public demands, 61, 62
Criteria weighting, numerical system,
94, 95
CRT, 95
CSI Format, 4, 7

Databanks, 90, 95, 103, 119
Decision-making, mental process, 63
performance criteria, 85
research, 64
systems approach, 64-68, 76
Decision-making process, client's involvement, 124
Decision-making program, 65-68
Design, affects of lifestyle changes,
60
Design changes, due to life style, 59
Design decisions, documented, 127
Designer's responsibility, 65-68, 98-
100, 111, 120
Design professional, client expectations, 98, 99
client interaction, 110
consultant interaction, 111
and design team, 111
and drafting team, 113
future role, 102
interaction with manufacturer and
contractor, 113
legal responsibilities, 103-106
liabilities, 61, 62
public demands, 61, 62
and specifier, 112
team work activities, 100
Design responsibilities, 60
Documented design decisions,
127

Documented information, 85, 102,
107, 121

Employee-training programs, 118
Environmental codes, 80
Evaluation matrix, 117
Evaluation process, systematic, 110

Federal Specifications standards, 4
Federal Specification test methods,
27, 44
Feedback programs, 70
Field checklist, 46, 47
Field information, recording,
standard procedures, 70
Field performance feedback pro-
grams, 115
Field representative, 125

Guarantee, 122

Historic data file, 127, 130
Historic performance data, documented, 121
Human performance requirements,
79

IDAC Project Information Clearing-
house, 68
Impact variables, matrix, 108
Information, documented, 64, 85,
102, 103, 107, 121
historic data banks of, 85
management, 118
organization, 68, 118
system, 69, 118
systematic organization of, 69
Information availability, 64
Information collection system, 68
Information Handling Service, 68
Information handling systems, 95
Information identification, 107
Information identification process,
68
Information library, 82

Information matrix, 125
  performance criteria, 129
  performance requirements, 129
  systematic approach, 126
Information program, 118
Information relationships, use of
  matrix, 86
Information retrieval, 103, 107
Information system, construction, 68,
  69
  in-house program, 69
Information utilization, 107
In-house design programs, 95
In-house education programs, 118,
  126
In-house programs, information
  system, 69
Installation, materials, 45, 47
  products, 45, 47
  systems, 45
Insurance ratings, 83
  building materials, 110
Interaction matrix, 107
Interaction network, 107

McGraw-Hill Information Systems
  Company, 68
Management program, 118
Manufacturer's representative, 113
Manufacturers, liabilities, 61, 62
  public demands, 61, 62
Manufacturer specifications, 124
Maslow's theory on human needs, 79
Master builder, 117
Master Builder concept, 57
Material evaluation, 4, 16
Material evaluation process, 118
Material evaluation programs, 95
Material failures, 119
Material installation, 45, 47
Material manufacturer, 128-130
Material performance, 78, 128
  environmental factors, 79
Material performance criteria, sys-
  tematic approach, 118

Material product evaluation,
  benefits of computer program,
  95
Material product selection, benefits
  of computer program, 95
Materials, new, 4
  performance aspects, 58
Material selection, 4, 16, 85, 112
  performance requirements, social
  and economic constraints, 80
  systematic approach, 108
Material selection process, 118
  problem analysis, 78
  systematic, 115
Material service program, 123
Materials investigation, 32
Material use, historic account, 53
Matrix, 16, 18, 86, 90, 108, 125, 129
  building performance criteria, 126
  computerized evaluation, 94, 95
  evaluation, 117
  graphic, 87
  interaction, 107
  manual evaluation, 94, 95
  performance criteria, 117, 121
Military research programs, 77
Monitoring programs, 70

National Technical Information
  Service, 68
Natural materials and synthetic
  products, performance comparison, 55
New materials, 4
  evaluation, 25, 26
  installation, 45
New products, evaluation, 24, 25, 44
  human performance, 55
  installation, 45
  selection, 44
New project, selecting a material, 26
  selection of materials, 25
  selection of products, 25
  selection of systems, 25
New system, evaluation, 25

Noncompliance statements, checklist, 129
Numerical weighting system, 117

Organized approach, development,
human capability, 76, 77
Overseas Building Note No. 23, 163

Performance characteristics, 39
Performance concept, 4, 24
Performance criteria, 82, 86, 88, 90,
94, 101, 102, 104, 107-109,
111-115, 118, 124, 126
building material evaluation, 120
building materials, 116
building material selection, 120
building products, 116
checklist, 129
compliance statement, 125, 126
compliance with, 122, 123
decision-making, 85
documenting, 82, 83
evaluation, 125
identification of, 81
information matrix, 129
matrix, 108, 117, 121
preparation, 83
specifications, 124, 125
systematic listing, 122
systematic quality control program, 128-130
technological capabilities, 83
weighting, 84-86
weighting system, 117
Performance criteria fulfillment, 125
records, 127
Performance criteria records, 123
Performance evaluation program,
final, 115
Performance levels, 25
Performance matrix, 129
Performance monitoring, 103
Performance records, 70
documented, 127
Performance requirements, 7, 16-18,
22, 24, 25, 81, 82, 89, 90, 105,

111, 114, 120
compliance statement, 125, 126
human, 79
information matrix, 129
material selection, social and economic constraints, 80
systematic quality control pro-
gram, 128-130
Product development, special re-
quirements, 89
Product development criteria, 129
Product evaluation programs, 95
Product failures, legal problems, 119
Product installation, requirements,
45, 129
Production Systems for Architects and
Engineers, Inc., 68
Product performance, 78
environmental factors, 79
recording of field information, 70
Product performance records, 127
Product research, 103
Product selection, 42
systematic approach, 108
Product service program, 123
Product standard, 4
Project evaluation, before and during
construction, 114, 115

Quality-control programs, 84

Research information, 103
Research organizations, 23
privately established, 72
Research programs, building ma-
terial, 71, 72
Retrieval systems, 64, 116

Selection criteria, 114
Showcase Corporation, 68
"Siporex," materials investigation, 32
Specifications, 124
Specifiers, 112
Standard test method references, 27
Statement of compliance, 122
Steel, 53

Synthetic products, 54, 55
Synthetic products and natural materials, performance comparison, 55
Systematic approach, 107, 120-122
 building design process, 117
 building material performance, 127,,
 128
 decision-making, 65-68, 76
 identification of building and material performance criteria, 118
 information matrix, 126
 legal implications for developing,
 126
 legal implications of using, 119
 performance criteria, 122
 product and material selection, 108
 selection of building materials, 75
 techniques for developing, 73
 time and cost savings, 127
 user needs, 81
Systematic evaluation process, 110
Systematic material selection
 process, 115
Systematic quality control program,
 128-130
System development, based on areas
 of impact, 78
 objectives of program, 75
 goals of program, 75

System installation, 45

Team work requirements, communi-
 cation, 100-102
 cooperation, 101, 102
 coordination, 101, 102
Technical data, library of, 118, 119
Technical information, library of, 118
Technological capabilities, perform-
 ance criteria, 83
Technological changes, 59
Technological problems, impact, 60
Technology, impact, 59
Turner Construction Company, field
 checklist, 46

U.S. Army Construction Engineering
 Research Laboratory, 69
User needs, 78, 79
 systems approach, 81

Warranty, 122
Waterproofing, 40, 43, 44
 performance characteristics, 39
 product selection, 42-44
Waterproofing materials, selection of,
 41
Weighting system, numerical, 117
 performance criteria, 117
Word processing systems, 95